SELLING PROFESSIONAL SERVICES

— THE —

SANDLER WAY

Or: "Nobody Ever Told Me I'd Have to Sell!"

CHUCK & EVAN POLIN

Sandler Training

SELLING PROFESSIONAL SERVICES
THE SANDLER WAY
Or: "Nobody Ever Told Me I'd Have to Sell!"

ISBN: 978-0-9832614-5-2

Visit us at www.sandler.com to learn more!

SELLING
PROFESSIONAL
SERVICES
—— T H E ——
SANDLER
WAY

To Helene, Caryn, and Jake for your motivation and inspiration.

To David H. Sandler for creating the best business development process the world has ever seen.

To our clients, friends, and strategic partners for your loyalty and support through the years.

TABLE OF CONTENTS

PART THREE: A SYSTEMATIC APPROACH TO DEVELOPING BUSINESS

PART FOUR: PUTTING IT ALL TOGETHER

ACKNOWLEDGEMENTS

None of this would have been possible without Helene Polin, a great life partner, mother, and business partner. Helene is the backbone of our organization and has put in countless hours of work throughout the entire process of writing this book. Our gratitude also goes out to Jamie and the incredible team at Sandler Training Philadelphia, Pennsylvania; to the Sandler Home Office for their support, particularly David Mattson for his guiding vision for Sandler Training; and to Yusuf Toropov and Brad Boesen for helping us pull this project together. Special thanks are also due to Steve Goodman from Morgan Lewis & Bockius and Jason Vermillion from Accenture for their valuable feedback and insight on the content of this project.

Last but not least, we want to express our appreciation to the clients who have worked with us over the past two decades for their friendship and support. We have thoroughly enjoyed working with all of you through the years, and we could not have done any of this without you.

FOREWORD

I f you're a professional reading these words, you've probably already dedicated a significant portion of your life to higher and continuing education, to certification in your discipline of choice, and to keeping up with the countless changes in your field. Let's face it — that's a lot of work, and it takes a lot of brainpower.

One day, though, you looked up from whatever you were working on, and you noticed that there were some people in your industry who were doing significantly better financially. Am I right?

So here's a question for you: Why?

Are they smarter than you? Probably not. They're just better at bringing in business than you. They're the rainmakers. If you've ever looked at the rewards they pull down and thought to yourself, "Why not me?" – please keep reading.

A popular myth has made the rounds for decades. Who knows from where it came? This myth undercuts, overstresses, and disempowers far too many people.

The myth I am speaking of holds that most of those who deliver specialized professional services — attorneys, accountants, consultants, engineers, architects, and all the rest — are temperamentally disinclined to sell effectively. Those who propagate this myth hold that there is an elite group of professionals called rainmakers who possess (apparently) supernatural skills in their (apparently) highly specialized discipline known as business development. These rainmakers, the story goes, have next to nothing in common with all the other professionals, at least concerning their mastery of those mysterious activities that win and retain clients.

This myth, the business equivalent of an urban legend, has become so prevalent that even a majority of the professionals themselves now believe it. In this book, Chuck and Evan Polin use the Sandler Selling System to debunk that myth forever.

Having worked with the Polins for decades, I can attest to the wisdom and the practical effectiveness of the selling system they have shared with thousands of professionals. That system assumes that the same skills that qualified professionals deploy each and every day — fact-finding, evaluating, prioritizing, qualifying, planning, and so on — can be leveraged, painlessly and without any embarrassment or discomfort, to build and expand a base of business. This approach has already worked for professionals all over the world — professionals who once firmly believed that they were not rainmakers and could not sell. And it can work for you.

Using the Sandler Selling System, any professional who has qualms about selling his or her services, or even about using the word "selling," can, with just a little practice and reinforcement over time, become a rainmaker. If you doubt that, then you're the person for whom the Polins wrote this book ... and my challenge to you is to start reading and applying the principles you will find laid out here.

If you do that, I predict that you will discover that all "selling" is really just communication ... that excelling at communication is well within your reach ... and that you can reap the same rewards enjoyed by the top people in your industry.

David Mattson
President/CEO, Sandler Systems, Inc.

CHAPTER ONE

"Nobody Ever Told Me I'd Have to Sell!"

"Why is business development my problem?"

Over the 20-plus years we have been in business, the number one complaint we hear from professionals — lawyers, accountants, engineers, consultants, and the like — has been this one:

"I did not go into this field to become a salesperson."

In other words, "Nobody ever told me I needed to build up a base of business."

Other common refrains we hear are:

"People should already know about my good work — so why should I have to worry about selling my services to anyone?"

"I am too busy providing the work. I have no time to go out and develop business!"

"I am no good at this."

Unfortunately, our educational system does not teach professionals how to build a practice. There are virtually no classes that teach professionals the techniques needed to build a book of business. Even in today's continuing education classes, very little time is devoted to business development. In fact, many of the professionals we work with are not even aware that they will need to develop business until they are several years into their career!

Fortunately, there is some good news, too.

> Even though you did not go into this line of work to become a salesperson or to worry about building up or expanding your base of business, and even though you think you are not good at it, you can use the strengths that you already have and use on a daily basis, along with some easy-to-learn new skills, to achieve or exceed your business and professional goals.

Some professionals we work with are naturally able to build their practice up to a certain level of success, but are looking to develop new systems and implement new ideas to continue their success within a changing economy, or to help take them and their business to the next level.

Other successful professionals are tasked with leading a team that has a few high-producing professionals who are experts at developing new business — and a few team members who have not yet managed to adopt the best practices of the top performers.

Some firms that have multiple practice areas find that some of their practice groups are more successful than other practice groups, and they are looking for strategies to make every part of their firm profitable.

This book will address all of these situations. Not only that, it will also show you how you can use your existing skill base to do it.

Here is our promise: If you are good at the other aspects of your career and you have the desire to develop business, you can be good at business development, too.

WHY SELLING PROFESSIONAL SERVICES MATTERS MORE THAN EVER

Years ago, having difficulty developing a book of business was not as big of a problem for professionals as it is today.

Before the early 1990s, clients were more loyal to the professional firms they chose, and less likely to jump ship, than they are today. It was not uncommon for accounting firms, consulting firms, law firms, and other professional practices to pass clients down from generation to generation. Many partners would inherit a book of business from the retiring partners, making it less important for newcomers to be able to develop a new client base. As a general rule, those loyal clients would not constantly shop around your services over rate issues either.

Times have changed! And if you do not change along with them — well, you are not going to enjoy yourself or have as much control over your career as you deserve.

Believe it or not, you can enjoy this. How? By taking skills you already enjoy deploying, and deploying them in a slightly different way. Sound interesting? Read on.

"WHY SHOULD I LISTEN TO YOU?"

You should listen to us because we have a long track record, because we have a process that works, and because we watch our clients successfully implement these ideas on a daily basis. At the end of the day, you should listen to us because we provide professional services ourselves, and because we have a nice, full book of business. In other words, we practice what we preach, and it works for us and it has been working for our clients for the last twenty years. So if you are not completely satisfied with the results that you are currently experiencing, it is time to listen to someone who has helped thousands of professionals who were right where you are — before they started working with us.

TRUE STORY: FRANK'S DILEMMA

People often ask us: How did we get into the practice of training professionals to develop business? Here is the answer.

CASE IN POINT

Approximately 20 years ago, one of our top sales training clients, a financial advisor, referred us to his top client, who happened to be the managing partner of a mid-sized law firm. The managing partner, Frank, faced a dilemma, and our client thought that we could help him.

Frank was in his mid-sixties; he was hoping to retire in a few years.

He wanted to map out his exit strategy, and he began that process by having his practice valued. The valuation revealed that he himself generated roughly 90 percent of the business for the firm. As a result, he was told his firm had almost no value if he was not there to develop business!

It was at this point that Frank knew that he needed to teach the attorneys in his firm to bring in their own book of business — or he would not be able to retire!

When we first met with Frank, we saw immediately that many of his challenges were precisely the same challenges that we were helping traditional sales organizations overcome. For instance, the attorneys who were trying to develop new business were haphazard at best in their approach. Many of the attorneys simply did not believe that bringing in new business was part of their job. The managing partner would tell the other attorneys to "just do what I am doing," but that did not seem to work.

The other attorneys did not have the relationships that Frank had, and no matter what Frank did or said, they developed little or no new business. What is more, many of the attorneys who worked at his practice flat-out did not believe that they had a "natural ability" to develop business, which is something they believed Frank did possess. Frank's associates believed that they were too busy practicing law to develop business, and they felt discouraged when their limited attempts to develop business did not lead to immediate tangible results.

As we dug a little deeper into Frank's practice, we discovered some sobering facts.

For instance: The attorneys were leaving thousands of dollars of easy business on the table. They were not asking for referrals because they did not know how to ask in a professional manner. They were not leveraging their relationships and contacts to create conversations about cross-selling or up-selling within their existing accounts. Last but not least, they were providing far too much free consulting for prospects who did not work with their firm.

Does any of this sound familiar?

It sounded familiar to us. As we began working with Frank, we adapted the classic Sandler Selling System® approach to meet the specific requirements of the attorneys who worked in his practice.

Within three years, he was able to retire!

ANOTHER TRUE STORY: THE YOUNG RAINMAKERS

This book is intended, first and foremost, as a resource for professionals who provide great day-to-day work for clients — but who are hesitant about taking on the responsibility of developing business for their firm. Sandler Training has worked with tens of thousands of such people.

CASE IN POINT

One of Sandler's clients is a very large consulting firm that services Fortune 500 clients. Most of the younger consultants in that firm were spending almost 100 percent of their time servicing their clients and had never been asked to develop new business for the firm. We have helped them to change that pattern, and the result has been dramatically better income performance across the firm — and higher income for the consultants!

The key to making that kind of change was not merely tactical. There were behavioral and attitudinal changes to process, too. For many professionals who find themselves in the same position those young consultants found themselves in, it can be very difficult to transition your mindset from one of "servicing the client" to the mindset that makes growing the firm's business a major priority. Often, the senior members of the firm are in a different stage in their career than an associate or young partner, and the tactics that the more senior partners employ to develop business are not appropriate, or simply uncomfortable, for the younger members of the firm. That was the case here. We opened up some new discussions, shared some new strategies, and helped to create a new generation of rainmakers.

The tactics and techniques shared in this book will help you develop your own personal business development process — using a style that works for you.

NO MORE FREE CONSULTING!

Another challenge that virtually all professionals must overcome when developing business is the "free consulting trap."

CASE IN POINT

An engineering firm had run into some major business development challenges. Senior executives were confused as to why the firm was not more profitable. The firm had won its fair share of large jobs. Where was the margin? They agreed to meet with Sandler to discuss the problem.

We sat down with the leadership of the firm, and we asked them some questions. First, we asked how often they needed to bid competitively on work in order to win projects. The senior leaders of the firm were not quite sure, but they knew that most of the business came through bid work.

Next, we asked if they had any idea of what percentage of the work that they bid on actually became clients. Again, they were not sure at first. They went back through their numbers and determined that 20 percent of the projects that they bid on developed into projects.

We then asked the firm's leadership how many "man-hours" it took to complete a bid. Once again, they had to go back and track the numbers. We eventually learned that it took approximately 100 man-hours to complete a single bid! Think about that: two and a half weeks of one professional's time to develop a bid that failed 80 percent of the time.

There was more. Along the way, there were plenty of so-called "networking" and "fact-finding" meetings that provided insights and experience that prospects benefited from, but for which prospects never paid. At Sandler, we call that kind of work "free consulting" — and in this case that is literally what it was.

Can you guess what we asked next? Correct. We asked them to track the hourly rate of the people who worked on the proposals.

Once all of the math was completed, it was determined that in just one quarter, this engineering firm had spent over *one million dollars* submitting bids on projects that they did not win!

It gets worse. As they looked at the profitability of the projects they were winning, they found that the margin was less than ten percent. Translation: Even when they were winning work, they were winning it based on a low bid and were not making much money!

There was no longer any mystery as to why that firm needed help with their business development process! We helped them turn around the "free consulting" habit, and both their revenue and their margins improved within just one calendar year.

SCALING BEST PRACTICES

Other firms are on the opposite end of the spectrum. They have been very successful in developing business, but they need to develop systems and processes to provide a foundation for more of the professionals in the firm to begin to generate new business at a higher level. Other firms we have worked with have had a good deal of success building their business up to a certain level, but had to change their strategy and their tactics to take their business to the next level.

CASE IN POINT

Recently, we gave a talk to an Alumni Association of a prominent college in the northeastern United States. This college invited back all of their graduates in the area who went on to attend law school. This was a special alumni event. We participated in a panel discussion about business development for attorneys. As part of our presentation, we asked the attorneys in attendance how many classes they took in law school on business development. The answer we received was "zero"!

There were over 100 practicing attorneys who had graduated from one dozen different law schools, and *not one had taken a course that taught him how to grow and build a practice*. We went on to ask how many of their continuing education courses were focused on building a practice, and the answer to that question was also "zero."

WHAT IS YOUR PLAN?

Our experience is that when it comes to business development, professionals utilize one of two systems. One of those systems is called "winging it," and the other system is called "flying by the seat of their pants." When you get right down to it, they are the same system — no system at all!

In later chapters, we will show you a proven approach for developing an effective professional business development plan and provide you with a process to systematically qualify opportunities. We will discuss what keeps professionals from moving out of their "comfort zone," which prevents them from changing their approach to business development. We will walk you through the steps of this process so that by the end of this book, you will have a roadmap of strategies to develop new business. This book is the start of a learning process. You will be given the tools to start on your journey to more effective business development practices. Note, though, that it will take time for you to practice and master the art of business development.

In the next chapter, we will discuss stepping out of your Comfort Zone.

Recap: Top Seven Reasons Why It Is Important to Develop Business

1. Developing business gives you more control over your career.
2. Developing business makes you more valuable to your current firm.
3. Developing business enables you to earn more money over the course of your career.
4. Developing business provides you with the opportunity to do the type of work that you enjoy doing.
5. Developing business helps you to get out of the office.
6. Developing business makes you a more well-rounded professional.
7. Developing business can actually be fun!

Recap: Top Seven Excuses for Not Developing Business

1. "I went into this field because I did not want to sell."
2. "I do not have time to develop business."
3. "I am not comfortable developing business."
4. "Nobody ever showed me how to develop business."
5. "I tried to do it once and I was not good at it."
6. "That is somebody else's job."
7. "I am really good at what I do. People should just know to call me if they need something."

CHAPTER TWO

The Comfort Zone

"What is the comfort zone?"

S ome say that the definition of insanity is doing the same thing over and over again and expecting different results.

At Sandler, we meet a lot of professionals who take what seems like an insane approach to business development: they keep right on doing what does not work.

When it comes to expanding your base of business, you will find that the concepts we teach are not very complex. You will find that the biggest business development challenge you face is not mastering some complex new concept, but rather changing your current behavior patterns and thought processes in order to use simple ideas to get different results.

Truth be told, it is difficult for most people to make even simple changes. Most of us, even if we are very successful, get caught in what we at Sandler call a "comfort zone."

Comfort zone: A behavioral space where your activities are consistent with your existing competencies, meaning your knowledge, skills, experiences, and abilities. Operating in your comfort zone minimizes stress and risk — but also limits growth.

SHAKING UP THE STATUS QUO

Here is a true story about someone who found himself caught in a comfort zone.

CASE IN POINT

Pete is an architect. Long before we started working with Pete, he saw that he had a need to make changes and move out of his comfort zone. Pete decided to begin the process by making one very simple behavioral change. When Pete drove out of his neighborhood every day, he had a choice to make a right turn or a left turn. Both of these turns took him to exactly where he needed to go in the same exact amount of time, but for some reason Pete always made a right turn.

Pete decided that he wanted to make small behavioral changes, and he started with something as seemingly insignificant as making a left turn during his morning commute instead of making a right turn. Pete found that it took about 90 days for this change to become a comfortable one. Every day for the initial 89 days, his impulse was to make a right turn!

It was not until 90 or more days that making a left turn felt natural to him. If it is that difficult to take a different route out of your neighborhood every day, imagine how difficult it can be to make major changes in your business behaviors that might be uncomfortable for you!

In order to change and grow, both personally and professionally, you will need to modify your behavior and do things a little differently than you have become accustomed to up until now. You will need to alter some familiar, preconceived ideas about what is appropriate, how you perceive your role and your value, how prospective clients think and act, what people will think of you, and most importantly, what you are capable of accomplishing.

You must dedicate yourself to new thoughts and actions for 90 or more days before you begin to internalize new messages. It takes dedication, commitment, persistence, and focus to make real emotional and behavioral change. Our experience is that the most successful change is internally driven. If you have a strong internal motivation to accomplish new goals, it will be easier for you to change your comfort zone than if you are only being "forced" to change by external factors.

We recommend a training routine that includes both internal motivation and external support, one that incorporates ongoing reinforcement. This is how adults learn best.

A GOOD PLACE TO START

The best place to begin when trying to change patterns and behaviors is to get a clear understanding of just what it is that affects motivation. At Sandler, we hold that there are two components that have an impact on what people actually do with their lives and their careers. Let us look at the first of those two parts now.

The core of who we are as a person is Identity. Our identity is who we really are.

> Your Identity is who you are. This is expressed through your core values, your beliefs, your ethics, your morals, and your view of the world.

If you feel good about your identity, that means you have a strong sense of self-worth. People who have a strong sense of self-worth do not worry about what the outside world thinks of them. They are resilient and are able to handle rejection. They are willing to take risks, and they perceive "failure" (notice the quotation marks) as a lesson learned and as an opportunity to grow.

By contrast, people who do not have a strong sense of self-worth are more susceptible to large mental and emotional swings when things do not go as planned. Professionals who have low self-worth might allow a bad meeting to turn into a bad day, which then can turn into a bad week leading to a bad quarter.

If we were to look at your identity on a scale of one to ten, where do you think your Identity falls right now? Did you write down a weak number one, a strong number ten, or did you fall somewhere in between? *Write your answer on a separate sheet of paper right now.*

Earlier, we said that there were two factors likely to affect motivation. The other component is our Role. Our Roles are what we do, the different "hats" that we wear day-in and day-out.

Now consider this: Baby boys are typically given blue blankets and baby girls are typically given pink blankets. Growing up, little boys are typically given cars, trucks, action figures, and sporting equipment, while little girls are often given dolls, jewelry, and more delicate toys. When we attend school, we find there are cliques like jocks, nerds, stoners, and troublemakers. All of this connects to roles we play!

> Your Roles are the different "hats" you wear during the course of your day: parent, friend, spouse, guitar player, partner, and so on.

As adults, we may play the role of parent, spouse, sibling, child, provider, or home maker. In the professional world, you might be a rainmaker, a subject matter expert, a board member, an administrative assistant, a bill collector, or a member of a firm. On any given day, we may perform better in some of those roles than we do in others.

ROLE VS. IDENTITY

What did you write down when we asked you to rate your identity on a scale from one to ten? (By the way, if you have not done that yet, please do it right now.)

We find that the most successful professionals, those who have a strong positive sense of their own identity, do not allow their role performance on any particular day to impact their identity. Typically, top performers give themselves a ten when asked to rate their identity! No matter how poorly they may perform as a guitar player, a subject matter expert, a tennis player, or anything else, they consider their core identity to be a ten on a scale of ten. That makes sense because each of us really is whole and complete as a human being!

Those professionals who have a lower self-worth, by contrast, will tend to take it personally when problems arise during the work day. Often, a professional in this group will not be willing to take any risks, will not take personal responsibility if goals are not achieved, and will not be accountable if problems arise with client work.

We have worked with a number of professional service firms who had members of their team simply refuse to participate in training and coaching around business development. We have even heard from some managing partners of law firms and accounting firms who told us that some of their professionals have threatened to leave the firm if they were expected to develop business. We have also spoken with many leaders of firms who are deeply frustrated because of conversations with professionals who volunteered to take pay cuts rather than move out of their comfort zone and try to learn how to develop new business for the firm!

THE BIG TAKEAWAY

What conclusions can we draw from reactions like these? Here is one: If people allow the outside world to affect the way that they feel about their identity *as a human being*, it becomes more difficult for them to take risks and move out of their comfort zone.

If people with low self-esteem take a risk and do not get the results they were looking for, it will be much less likely for them to take a second risk. In addition, if they do take a risk that does not work out, they are likely to allow that failure to impact other aspects of their work.

CLOSE-UP: THE WINNER PSYCHOLOGICAL POSITION

At Sandler, we believe that people fall into three psychological positions – the At-Leaster psychological position, the Winner psychological position, and the Loser psychological position.

To make this conversation easier, picture a scale that ranges from one to ten, where ten is the top score, and one is the bottom.

IDENTITY POSITIONS

Identity	Role	
10	10	
9	9	
8	8	WINNER Position
7	7	
6	6	
5	5	AT-LEASTER Position
4	4	
3	3	
2	2	LOSER Position
1	1	
0	0	

On this scale, the person in the Winner psychological position shows up at seven, eight, nine, or ten. This person has high self-esteem, feels good about himself most of the time, and takes responsibility for his own actions as well as their results. The person in the Winner psychological position is willing to take risks, and if he does not succeed, he will accept his "failures" as learning opportunities, so that he can be in a better position the next time he takes a risk. This professional is constantly trying to learn new things and to better himself. A very small percentage of the general population falls into this category!

CLOSE-UP: THE AT-LEASTER PSYCHOLOGICAL POSITION

The person in the At-Leaster psychological position ranges from four to six on our scale. This professional is comfortable with average performance, although hearing him actually say so is rare. The way these people feel about themselves is tied to past role performance; they tend to resist stretching out of their comfort zone. People in the At-Leaster mindset will provide consistent work, but they will not stretch outside of their comfort zone and will avoid putting themselves in situations where they might fail or need to change. People in the At-Leaster psychological position content themselves with the fact that they will never be a poor performer. They want to avoid being singled out as below average, but at the same time, they will not overachieve. Why? Because they are afraid someone will expect outstanding performance from them all of the time!

For organizations that have quotas or goals, it is easy to spot the professionals who operate within the At-Leaster mindset. In our experience, those with the At-Leaster mindset who hit their monthly quota three weeks into the month will spend the last week of the month on the golf course (literally or figuratively)! If additional deals come in, they will actually hold those deals so they can be put towards the next month's quota. This is the At-Leaster mindset in action. Whether they realize it or not, people in this group choose not to overachieve because they do not want to have to live up to high expectations on a regular basis.

You will also find that many professionals in this category will be content serving the same accounts and selling the same services over and over again — but when they are asked to open up new opportunities or cross-sell services they are not familiar with, they are likely to become uncomfortable and resist the new activities, even if these activities represent significant new income potential.

Our experience is that much of the population falls into the At-Leaster psychological position.

CLOSE-UP: THE LOSER PSYCHOLOGICAL POSITION

The person operating in the Loser psychological position falls between a three and a one on the Identity/Role chart.

The Loser psychological position correlates with low self-esteem; people in this group allow their role performance to affect how they feel about themselves. Professionals with this mindset do not take responsibility for either successes or failures.

The person in the Loser psychological position rarely takes responsibility for a lack of results, and if something goes wrong, this person is likely to say that it is somebody else's fault. Typically, the professionals we run into who work within the Loser psychological position will not try *any* new things on the job because they have the belief that they cannot succeed. In addition, they tend to surround themselves with other people who have the same beliefs and thought processes.

Unfortunately, there are far more people in this world with the At-Leaster or Loser mindset than with the Winner mindset.

The whole idea behind this book is to help you move up this scale toward the Winner position. That means moving out of your comfort zone! In order to move out of your comfort zone, you will need to foster new attitudes and beliefs. You will have to re-think and realign your "Identity" position — and as a result, your "Role" performance will improve.

MOVING TOWARDS THE "WINNER" POSITION

You can break through your comfort zone with new behaviors and supportive attitudes. You can make the decision to move beyond your comfort zone right now! Take a quick break. Start creating a written plan that identifies at least one specific area where you want to improve in terms of business development. Arrange to get help and support in the form of an accountability partner with whom you can share honest discussions about mutual goals.

CASE IN POINT

One of our clients is an attorney named Mary. Mary came to us because most of her business had come from one large client, and through no fault of hers, that client no longer needed her services. When we began to work with Mary, she fell into the At-Leaster psychological position. Mary had good intentions and knew that she needed to change, but she was afraid to take risks and move out of her comfort zone. When we started working with Mary, she was willing to try new things, but it was a very slow process. Over the course of several months, and after much discomfort, Mary became more involved with different business development activities and began to work her prospecting plan. After nine months of trying new tactics and moving out of her comfort zone, Mary tripled her book of business from the previous year. She is now actively networking, and, as a result, she now requires help from other attorneys in her firm to service the new business that she has generated!

In the next chapter, we will look at how to get started.

 **SANDLER® RULE** You can perform in your roles only in a manner that is consistent with how you see yourself conceptually.

CHAPTER THREE

How Do I Get Started?

"Why should I take time away from the things I do best?"

Most professionals who successfully develop business do not become successful by accident. There may be a very small percentage that "gets lucky" and "falls into" a large account or a great relationship — leaving these professionals vulnerable in the event that business ever disappears. This is why everyone, even those who are fortunate enough to inherit important accounts, should design a plan and work that plan in order to develop new business.

MAKE A DECISION

The first step in successfully developing business is a deceptively simple-sounding one. You must decide for yourself that you really do want to engage in the business development process.

Developing new business takes hard work, a willingness to try something new and risk failure, and the ability to move out of your comfort zone. These requirements prevent many from deciding with full intention that they are willing to engage in the process.

Two Commitments

Specifically, there are two major commitments you must make in order to be successful in business development.

The first is a time commitment. In chapters four through fifteen we will discuss the steps of executing a successful business development plan, a large part of which relies on committing yourself to spending a specific amount of time *working* your plan. For some people, it is possible to be successful developing business in as a little as four to five hours per week. Other professionals may need to make a larger time commitment to develop the base of business they need. Either way, if you want to be successful, you must commit some time to prospecting, cultivating relationships, and meeting with potential clients.

The next commitment takes the form of a willingness to change current practices that simply do not work. Very few of the professionals that we meet are developing more business than they or their firm can handle. That means just about everyone has room to improve, and just about everyone is doing something that is not working as well as it could.

If you want to develop more new business, you must change your mindset as well as your behaviors. And, as we have noted, in order to achieve success, you must *want* to develop new business. For most of the professionals we work with, this is a major change.

There is no book or training program that will help the professional who has no interest in changing. You will need to look at business development in a whole new light, change the way you approach the task of scheduling your day, your week, and your month, and then actually try some new activities and new techniques. If you have already been successful developing business, you may need to move into new markets, reach out to new contacts, or implement new tactics to achieve the next level of success. If you are successful selling some of your services or practice areas but not others, you may need to look at what changes need to be made in the underperforming areas.

A willingness to embrace change is also essential for professionals who hold leadership positions in the firm. For instance: If you have tasked your most successful business development people and rainmakers with the responsibility of mentoring other, less successful members of the firm, but have not seen positive results arise from that mentoring, you may need to look at developing a different system or process that will help more of the people in your firm to generate new business.

One major behavioral change that just about everyone we work with has to come to terms with is that of preparing and practicing an answer to the common requests, "Tell me about yourself" and "Tell me about your business." In chapter ten, you will learn about the 30-Second Commercial, which is a memorable way for you to introduce yourself to someone you have not previously met. For most professionals, the format we use is radically different from the 30-second commercials they have tried in the past. In all likelihood, you will need to practice your new 30-second commercial 50 to 100 times before becoming comfortable enough with it to deliver it naturally to a new acquaintance.

BREAKING THE INSANITY CYCLE

We can assure you that there is only one time when the tactics and techniques that we will share with you here do not work. *They do not work when you do not try them.*

In our 20-plus years of working with business professionals, we find that 10-15 percent of the professionals we have worked with are simply unwilling to move out of their comfort zone and try out new ideas. We hear things from the skeptics like, "This will not work for me," or "This will not work in my business." But when we ask them for the reasons *why* they believe these tactics and techniques will not work, they cannot give us an answer.

The truth is that some people are so rooted in their current comfort zone that it is almost impossible for them to change. Remember, the definition of insanity is doing the same things over and over and expecting different results. Our challenge to you is to break this insanity cycle so you can obtain the results you need in your business development endeavors.

YOU GET WHAT YOU PAY FOR

In addition to what you have just read, you and your firm must make a financial commitment to business development. Professionals who have the most success developing business hire some type of coach to work with them in improving their skills. Hiring an outside expert is only logical. Most of our clients have invested tens to hundreds of thousands of dollars in completing their formal professional training in their chosen field. They have attended college, graduate school or law school, conferences and seminars, and they have invested in ongoing continuing education.

It should come as no surprise, then, that the most successful professionals, the ones who are the most productive business developers and rainmakers, make a financial investment in themselves. They commit to providing themselves with the tools they need to be successful.

THE FOUR-STEP PROCESS

There is a four-step process that we suggest you follow in order to be truly successful in business development. The steps are laid out below.

1. Ask for Help

The first step is to engage with an individual coach who can help you hone your business development skills. The most successful athletes and business professionals always receive individual coaching. Your coach should help you set up and customize your plan, help you modify your plan as needed, and hold you accountable for executing your business development plan.

2. Do an Assessment

The next step of this process is to invest in a assessment tool, so that you can determine your natural strengths and weaknesses when it comes to business development. There are over 25 different business development activities that might be appropriate for you and your market, and at least one of them makes sense for you. (We recommend the DISC or Devine assessment to our clients.) When you complete your assessment, your coach can customize a business development plan specifically tailored to your needs, strengths, and personal style. We find that ten different professionals within a firm may well need ten different business development plans, each based on their individual strengths and weaknesses.

3. Keep Learning

The third step of the four-step process is to engage in some kind of ongoing training for business development. As we have said before, many of the skills outlined in the pages that follow will take weeks or months for you to master.

We would suggest that after you complete this book, you look for additional resources that will help you to improve and expand your business development skills. After you learn these new skills, it will be important to put yourself in situations where you can utilize them. Finally, after you utilize the skills, you will need to notice what works and what does not — as well as what changes are in order for you to become more successful.

4. Track Your Results

The final step of the process is to track your results systematically. We will discuss ways of measuring Return on Investment (ROI) in more detail in chapter fifteen. For now, understand that if you are going to take the time to develop business, and if you are committed to investing money intelligently in your growth and skill development, you must be able to track and measure the results of your efforts. Before you even begin this measurement process, you should try to visualize what success actually looks like to you, and make sure that you understand the metrics that will help you determine your success or failure. Outside of overall revenue, what would you like to track? Is it the number of referrals you receive? The amount of revenue you generate from cross-selling and up-selling? Is it improving the profitability of your clients, shortening your selling cycle, or improving your closing percentage? Could it be all of the above?

In the next part of the book, you will begin to set up your prospecting plan. You will start by learning about SMART Goals, and then learn the steps you need to take in order to put together your business development plan.

Recap: Four-Step Process for Success in Business Development

1. Ask for Help
2. Do an Assessment
3. Keep Learning
4. Track Your Results

CHAPTER FOUR

Setting SMART Goals

"My goal is to serve my clients well. That should be enough, right?"

I n 1953, researchers at Yale University polled the graduating class and found that just three percent of the graduates had a set of clearly defined written goals.

Twenty years later, in 1973, these researchers re-visited the class of '53 and found that this same three percent, those graduates with written goals, had amassed a net worth that was greater than all of the other 97 percent combined.

This is a powerful indication that goal setting — meaning committing your goals to writing — is critical for success.

MAPPING YOUR COURSE

Earlier in this book, we discussed the two different plans that most professionals utilize when it comes to business development: "winging it" and "flying by the seat of your pants." Typically, when we ask professionals about their prospecting plans, we hear responses like, "I get referrals," or "I go to networking events." Rarely, if ever, do professionals share with us a well-thought-out prospecting plan. In the next few chapters, we will outline the steps for developing an effective prospecting plan.

Many professionals who work at larger firms will spend part of December building their business plan for the following year. When we ask questions about what is done with that plan once it is completed, one of two things happens: either we see a blank stare, or we are told that the plan is scheduled to be reviewed the following December, when it is time to implement the business plan for the next year.

If you want to be successful with business development, that outlook needs to change.

Focus!

The most successful professionals are the ones who are laser-focused when it comes to building and refining their business development plan. When setting goals, these clients set SMART goals.

The *S* in SMART Stands for *Specific*

When setting goals, you must be very specific about what it is that you would like to accomplish. Is there a number of new clients that you would like to develop? Do you have a revenue goal that you would like to hit? Do you want to increase profit margins? If so, by what percentage? If your goals are not specific, how are you going to know whether or not you are on track toward accomplishing them?

The *M* in SMART Stands for *Measurable*

Progress toward a goal must be quantifiable. Vague goals are demotivating and impossible to achieve.

CASE IN POINT

We once worked with an architect who told us that he wanted to "do better each year." When we asked him what "better" meant, he had a difficult time answering the question. We pressed him on the point, and finally, out of frustration, he said that if he did one dollar better each quarter, he'd be happy.

We then asked him another question. We asked this architect if his expenses increased by more than one dollar per quarter. He told us that his expenses increased much more than that. We then asked him what he thought about his previously stated goal.

He realized, of course, that a dollar increase in revenue every three months was not a SMART goal.

Our clients select a variety of factors to measure and track over the course of a year. They can measure success by looking at both leading and lagging indicators to measure success.

A leading indicator is a trackable behavior that will let you know if you are on the right path, such as appointments with new prospective clients, the number of times you have asked for a referral, the number of networking events that you have attended, or the number of meetings you have had with potential strategic partners.

Lagging indicators are the results that you can measure *after* you have completed the above behaviors, such as the number of closing appointments or proposals delivered, the number of new clients under contract, the number of referrals received, or the profit margin on the business that you are closing.

It is important, when setting goals, to be sure you are looking at both behavior *goals* and their *results*.

The *A* in SMART Stands for *Attainable*

When you set your goals, you should stretch outside of your current comfort zone. You want to make them "stretch goals." Yet you also want to balance that new stretch goal by making it a goal that you have a realistic chance to achieve. If you developed one million dollars in business last year, a ten-million-dollar goal for next year is probably not realistic. That goal is going to be demotivating — unless something has dramatically changed for the better within your business.

The *R* in SMART Stands for *Relevant*

Relevant means the goals you set are compatible with your other goals and do not conflict with them. If one of your goals is to rise to the top of your field, no matter what — and another goal is to spend more time with family — you are going to have a problem.

The goals you select must be aligned with your values and your personal aspirations. If they are not, you will eventually lose interest. Make sure that when you are setting your goals, you are considering your other goals and your own previous history. Set goals that truly make sense for you personally, not goals that just look good on paper.

The *T* in SMART Stands for *Time-bound*

There is a saying: a goal without a deadline is only a dream. One trap professionals fall into is that of constantly putting off their goals. They will state something that they would like to accomplish, but the due date is constantly pushed back. Does that sound familiar to you? Can you think of anyone who discusses big goals, but then keeps putting those goals off into the future?

To successfully set and achieve goals, you need to put a due date in place and do your utmost to honor that due date. After the due date is set, it is important to break the big picture goal into smaller pieces — and set deadlines for hitting these benchmarks along the way.

GOAL-SETTING WORKSHEET

GOAL:
_____
_____

FEARLESS INVENTORY – Where am I now?
_____
_____

ROADBLOCKS OR OBSTACLES
_____
_____

IS IT A S.M.A.R.T. GOAL?

___ SPECIFIC ___ MEASURABLE ___ATTAINABLE
___ RELEVANT __TIME-BOUND

GAME PLAN – "HOW AM I GOING TO DO THAT?"
_____
_____

HIGH PRODUCTIVE DAILY ACTIVITIES NEEDED TO "MAKE IT SO."
_____
_____

HOW BADLY DO I WANT IT? 1. 2. 3. 4. 5. 6. 7. 8. 9. 10.

Additional Suggestions

There are several other suggestions we can offer that will improve your chances of accomplishing your goals.

Write It Down

Once you have put SMART goals into place, make sure that you record those goals in writing. Our experience is that when people put their goals in writing, it makes them more accountable for achieving those goals.

After the goals have been written, it is important to look at them on a regular basis. Check in on your progress to determine whether or not you are actually moving towards your goals! Look at whether your leading indicators are being met, and check to see whether those leading indicators are really helping you to hit your goals. If they are, stay on plan and continue to implement the proper behaviors. If they are not, make sure that you tweak and change your behaviors, so that you can get back on track towards hitting your goals.

Tell Somebody

Next, make sure that you share your goals with the appropriate people. An "appropriate person" is someone who can hold you accountable!

Some people are mandated to review their goals with a supervisor or manager, and the process of sitting down and meeting with a supervisor or manager can indeed help with accountability. Others will choose a mentor or colleague whose opinion they value. That way they can get feedback on their goal, and receive suggestions about how to more effectively achieve them. Again, recall that most successful professionals will hire a coach to help hold them accountable for reaching their goals. A good coach will make sure you are executing your targeted behaviors on a regular basis — and give you advice on how to make constructive changes.

Look at the Big Picture

If you are part of a large organization, your goals also need to be aligned with the other parts of your organization. It is important to make sure that the goals of each department or practice group are in line with the goals of the overall organization. Each group needs to understand how what is happening fits into the firm's "big picture." In addition, make sure that everyone within your department understands not only the firm's vision for their practice area, but also their part in achieving those goals.

Make It Personal

Finally, we suggest that you tie something personal to the achievement of your goals — especially if your goals are being set for you by your firm or your company.

In the next chapter, we will talk about the various ways clients perceive you — and how you can change their point of view.

CASE IN POINT

Megan worked for a consulting firm that had given her an aggressive new business development goal. Megan had very little motivation or personal connection tied to that goal, and she had a difficult time getting motivated to achieve it. We suggested to Megan that she tie a personal reward to achieving that goal. When we met with her the next week, Megan had decided that if she achieved the goal that was set for her by her company, she would take her family on a trip to Disney World. Megan had been promising her family the trip for two years, but she was always too busy to make it happen.

At our suggestion, she also shared her goal with her family. By sharing her goal with her husband and three children, Megan enlisted the best accountability partners that a person could want. Every night when she came home from work, her three kids asked if they were getting closer to going to Disney World. Talk about pressure! Megan knew that if she did not complete her business development behavior each day, she would have three very upset children on her hands.

By the end of the third quarter, Megan had hit the goal that her boss set for her — and her family was able to make that trip to Disney World!

Recap: SMART Goals

S — SPECIFIC
M — MEASURABLE
A — ATTAINABLE
R — RELEVANT
T — TIME-BOUND

CHAPTER FIVE

Move from Vendor to Strategic Advisor

"How do I get clients to see me as more than just a provider?"

Many professionals say: "I generate referrals by doing my job well and by providing good client service. My time is better spent doing that than trying to find new clients on my own."

In fact, our clients *love* to tell us they develop all the clients they need, based entirely on their current business relationships. That seems to be the one thing on which they all agree. When we explore what they mean, we hear things like, "I get my prospects and strategic partners to like me, and then I get their business." Typically, those comments are followed by statements such as, "I get all of my business from referrals," or "My firm/company has been doing business with these clients forever."

In an ideal world, all the above statements would be true, and we would not need to prospect for new business. Unfortunately, experience tells a different story, a story of disconnect between those words and the reality. Every day, we speak with professionals who are frustrated that they have lost business because a competitor cut their rates, or because the "honeymoon" phase of the relationship ended unexpectedly, or because the person with whom they had a supposedly "long-term" relationship left the company unexpectedly, or because a buying decision got put off indefinitely.

This disconnect between the words and the reality is more notice-able today than it was a few decades ago. The dynamic of relationships with clients has changed over the years. Gone are the days where a client stays with a firm for decades without shopping out their rates to the competition. Clients are less and less likely to stay with a firm just because they have had a long-term relationship with a certain profes-sional or a certain firm. The result: Professional firms need to develop new business constantly, and they need to continue to show value to their current clients. They cannot depend on former clients to award them the work because the firm has "always" given them work in the past. It is imperative to make sure that your *current* clients see you as more than just a commodity, no matter how solid the relationship may seem, and no matter how much the client likes you.

Why? We choose to answer that question with a question. As you think about your own business, do you make important decisions based solely on whether you like someone, or do you make decisions based on what's best for your business right now?

Once you understand how you are viewed and how you deliver the perceived value that you bring to your client relationships, you can more effectively create strategies to develop long-term relationships with your clients — and keep a competitive advantage over the competition.

Prospects and clients can view you in one of three different ways: as a vendor, consultant, or strategic advisor. Let's look at each now.

"Vendor" Status

The lowest level is that of the vendor. A client who perceives your firm as a vendor views your relationship as transactional and interchangeable. If your rate or price is the cheapest, the client will do business with you. That's all. The moment another vendor presents the client with cheaper rates, or offers a newer, more exciting service — or catches your client after he did not receive an ideal outcome with you — the client who views you as a vendor will move to the competition.

When prospects put you in the vendor category, they will often use you for only one service, and they may be reluctant to refer you, even to people within their own organization. If you have ever had a client leave without warning, you can be sure that you were viewed as a vendor. If you have a current client who is constantly pushing you to cut your rates, you can be sure that client views you as a vendor.

First Impressions

Often, the way you are viewed by prospects or clients begins with the very first contact you have with them. So: Are you using the necessary strategies to be viewed at a high level by the prospects you are targeting, or does your first impression look and sound exactly like that of the competition? What are you doing to differentiate yourself and bring value to the relationship from the first moment onward?

Here is an example of what we mean. Over the years, we have worked with many law firms that provide work for banks. Banks are well known for treating their law firms like vendors and shopping for them solely based on rates. Typically, the banks will talk several times per year with their law firms about the importance of keeping their billing rates low. Banks will have ongoing talks with multiple law firms so that they can constantly push back on price with their current providers. Attorneys who are not able to show compelling additional value above and beyond their rate will find themselves fighting, on a regular basis, to hold onto clients by keeping rates low. This is a situation where you must find a way to leave a radically different impression from that of your competitors!

"Giving Away the Store"

Often engineering firms, architectural firms, and construction companies find themselves treated like vendors by their prospects. When a potential client has a new piece of work, that company will often "put the work out to bid." The potential client will use this process to obtain free consulting (including pricing) from many different companies. Too often, we find that firms are more than willing to provide free consulting before developing a relationship with their prospect. They imagine they are leaving a positive first impression. They are not.

Once the prospect has received free consulting from anxious vendors hoping to win the business, there will be a round of conversations with all of those "qualified bidders" about lowering their price. Because they look at these firms as vendors, prospects assume that everyone provides the same or similar levels of service, which is rarely the case. Once prospects choose a vendor, they call that vendor and ask for a best and final offer.

Companies and firms who never move beyond the vendor category not only have a hard time being profitable — they can have a difficult time staying in business.

"Consultant" Status

Those firms that are able to take their business relationships to the next level have more than a friendship with their clients. They develop a more trusting relationship that allows them to be viewed as a consultant.

In the business development world, a consultant is considered an expert in a specific industry. Clients perceive a consultant as a professional who is a more valuable team member than a vendor. Clients who view you as a consultant will ask for your expertise and advice in regards to your specialization when making decisions. They believe that you are more than a commodity and that you bring more to the relationship than just the role of a service provider. These clients typically will not complain about your rate or shop you around because they see the value that you bring to the relationship.

Typically, clients who view you this way will not leave you without a compelling reason. More often than not, they will share that reason with you, and it will not come as a surprise to you if a client does decide to move to one of your competitors.

The Upper Hand

Sometimes, when you are viewed as a consultant, you have some leverage if your clients try to treat you like a vendor and pressure you into lowering your rates.

CASE IN POINT

ABC is an insurance defense law firm. Typically, insurance defense firms are seen as vendors by their clients, and they are constantly being asked to reduce their rates. ABC came to us because a major client, a large insurance company, sent ABC a letter stating that there would be across-the-board, 15 percent cuts in the hourly rate that they were willing to pay. Our client was not sure what to do. ABC's attorneys provided thousands of hours of work for that insurance company each year, and the cut in rate would have cost them over $100,000 in revenue.

We asked senior partners of ABC whether they believed that the client was happy with their work, and the answer came back instantly that they were. There were multiple emails documenting that satisfaction. We suggested that ABC schedule a call with the insurance company to discuss the fee issues. During the call, we told ABC to share with the insurance company that their letter discussing rates was timely because ABC was about to send the insurance company a letter outlining an increase in rates for the upcoming year.

Initially, ABC was quite reluctant to take our advice, but after much urging from us they decided to call the insurance company. At first, the insurance company balked and threatened to move their business to another law firm. At our suggestion, ABC responded by asking where the files should be sent. They also asked the insurance company if they wanted to see the letters from their (the insurance company's) employees who talked about the good work that ABC was providing for the insurance company. They then asked the insurance company how long it would take for the new law firm to get up to speed with all of the files.

Because the insurance company valued the work that they were getting from ABC, the insurance company agreed that, rather than cutting the hourly rate, they would give ABC a raise of five percent. ABC was valued for its specialized expertise, and as a result, the partner who managed the relationship with that client negotiated a fee that was 20 percent higher than what the insurance company initially wanted to pay!

"STRATEGIC ADVISOR" STATUS

A strategic advisor is viewed by clients as a true business partner. It is rare for clients to view you as a strategic advisor, but when that happens, you will probably have a client for life.

Issues such as rates, new services, and pressure from your competitors will cease to exist when you are viewed as a strategic advisor. When your clients view you as an advisor, they ask you for advice. Often, they will share their future plans with you and seek your input. Clients who view you as a strategic advisor will be the strongest referral sources you could possibly hope for because they see you as an integral part of their business. These clients will be invested in your success, and they will usually do whatever it takes to help you grow your practice.

CASE IN POINT

To illustrate our point, let us tell you about a client who worked with our firm and came to perceive us as a strategic advisor. When we began working with this client, we were hired to train their sales force. When we completed this task, we were asked to train their management people. As we worked with this firm, we introduced them to four different law firms to handle four issues that required this firm's specialized expertise. We helped them to form a board of advisors and brought in someone to help them with their operations management. We were involved with every aspect of their business; we were viewed as a valuable strategic advisor.

It is much more difficult to develop the strategic advisor relationship than the consultant relationship. As the name strategic advisor suggests, trust is a major factor when trying to develop a strategic advisor relationship. Your client needs to know with certainty that you have their best interests in mind, and they must value your advice accordingly.

Typically, a strategic advisor has more meaningful relationships with clients than vendors or consultants. The strategic advisor will ask big picture questions such as, "Where do you see your business in five years?" and "What are your greatest obstacles to success?" — and the client will feel comfortable sharing major fears and concerns. By the same token, when your clients see you as a strategic advisor, they will ask you big picture questions and ask for your expertise in areas of importance to them.

Some of the accountants we work with who have strategic advisor relationships with their clients are asked to introduce the client to insurance professionals, legal professionals, bankers, and other business advisors. It is up to the strategic advisor to develop relationships that will be truly beneficial to clients in all areas of their business.

One accounting firm we worked with began working with a pharmaceutical company by doing only their tax work. As a result of this relationship, the accounting firm was hired to do the pharmaceutical company's SEC work and mergers and acquisitions work. Eventually the accounting firm was asked by the pharmaceutical company to refer them to legal counsel. Now the accounting firm sits on the board of advisors of the pharmaceutical company to help determine firm policy! Clearly, the accounting firm has been elevated to strategic advisor status.

STANDING OUT FROM THE CROWD

In these competitive times, it is important to differentiate yourself from the competition so that you can win — and, ultimately, keep — business. That means it is important to be aware of the manner in which your prospects and clients view you. Are you viewed as a vendor? Are you viewed as a consultant? How many of your clients view you as a strategic advisor? If you are not viewed as a strategic advisor as often as you would like, what are you going to do to change the nature of your relationship? When prospecting, how can you come across as a strategic advisor rather than a vendor? (By the way, you will learn more about that important topic in chapter ten.)

In the next chapter, we will discuss identifying appropriate business development targets.

Recap: Three Ways Clients Can Perceive You:

- Vendor
- Consultant
- Strategic Advisor

CHAPTER SIX

Developing Your Targets

*"Clients come to me, I do not go to them — so
how would I even know where to look?"*

Most professionals, and indeed most professional firms, simply
do not do a very good job of planning for success. They do
not put processes in place to help themselves and the firm to
grow. Since there is no plan in place for client development (or the plan
put in place is "for everyone," regardless of personal style, network size,
or experience) many professional service firms end up developing clients
more or less by accident. Some established firms rely on their firm's "good
name" in the hope that long-time clients will be loyal, and brand recognition alone will attract new clients. Unfortunately, that is not a sustain-
able business model. That business model does not allow your firm to
control its own destiny by proactively taking steps to build business!

This really is your problem. Whether you like it or not, whether you
came to this book on your own volition or as a result of the suggestion
of someone else, planning and building a client base is going to be a key
factor in determining your success. It is OK to be uncomfortable as you
begin the business development process or implement a new strategy —
it is not OK to ignore your business development responsibilities. *Right
now* is the time for you to learn the skills needed to build and grow

your book of business. Chief among those responsibilities is the task of developing a list of targets.

> To be truly successful and profitable in the long term, it is essential that you target the specific areas where you would like to grow your business.

DEVELOP A GAME PLAN FOR CLIENT DEVELOPMENT

Many professionals are uncomfortable developing business because they were never taught how to do it. Fortunately, business development skills, like other skills, can be learned, mastered, and sharpened. You already know, of course, that successful business people plan for their success, and that they *become* successful by developing and working a plan. This plan is just like any other plan you would develop on behalf of your career and/or your firm.

An effective business development plan begins with an understanding of your ideal client, meaning the kind of prospect you want to target. That sounds simple enough, but very often we find that professionals will chase after opportunities before they take a step back to determine exactly what they would like to accomplish, or whether the opportunities that happen to be in front of them fit into their long-term plan.

Find What Works

The first step for targeting clients is to look at the clients who you are working with currently. Which segments of your business are the most profitable? Which would you like to expand? In addition, you need to make sure that you have both a philosophy and a business process that you are following with your best current clients as you move to build up your client base.

Some firms are in the business of setting low margins on projects. They have the infrastructure to service many clients at one time. Such firms, when they are successful, can be profitable by producing low-margin work at high volumes. Other firms are set up so that they are quite limited in the number of projects that they can work on, but they are able to make a large profit from each project.

Those are the two ends of the spectrum. There is not a right or wrong model. The question that you need to ask yourself is, "Which model works best for me and my firm?"

Many of the firms that we work with offer multiple services. One mistake that we see firms make when targeting and setting their goals is that they set a goal for the overall revenue of the firm, but they do not break the goal down into their expectations for each individual practice area. In most firms, different practice areas and different services have different profitability levels. If you are able to sell services in one of your practice areas (even if that area is not quite as profitable as others), that might lead the way to selling additional services in other practice areas in the future.

Make sure that when you are looking to target new business, you do not limit yourself to looking for potential clients. You should also identify and target potential strategic partners and referral partners.

Ways to Target Clients

We can look now at some specific methods for targeting clients.

Vertical Markets

When you are targeting new clients, you may want to start the process by targeting vertical markets. Vertical markets are industry-specific, such as finance, manufacturing, healthcare, education, professional services, and IT.

One of the best ways to target vertical accounts is to look at the historical data for you and your firm. Are there specific industries or vertical markets that you have had a lot of success working with in the past? The key is to begin with industries where you have a history, and target those industries based on your expertise in that area.

Becoming involved with industry associations can help you to penetrate those vertical markets. For instance: An accounting firm that we worked with had an agricultural client in the mushroom industry and decided to go after other companies in that industry, since they already understood the nuances of the mushroom business. They solicited those companies by becoming active in the mushroom association and ended up with over a dozen new clients in that industry.

Client Size

Another way to target clients is by looking at client size. One attribute that we look at is the size of the engagements and the amount of revenue that a client may generate for your company or firm.

Small, Mid-Sized, and Large

What kind of business do you want to close, and from whom, over what period of time? The answer to this question should not be "anyone I run into."

It may be helpful to think of clients as coming in three different sizes: Small, Mid-Sized, and Large.

We call low-end clients (in terms of both profitability and revenue) the Small accounts. There is nothing wrong with Small accounts, but you do not want to try to build your entire income stream around them. Determine the number of Small accounts that you have the capacity to service over a given month, quarter, or year. In addition, you should determine the minimum amount of revenue that you need to collect from a Small account to ensure that servicing that client is worth your time.

There are also Mid-Sized clients in terms of the revenue that they generate for your firm over time. In addition to revenue, you probably want to look at the profitability of your client work when identifying a Mid-Sized client. These clients should produce revenue in areas that are more profitable for you and your firm than your Small clients. Determine what amount of revenue, for you and/or your firm, should be coming from Mid-Sized clients, as well as the total number of Mid-Sized clients that you will need in order to meet your goals for the coming month, quarter, or year.

The really Large clients are part of the picture as well, of course. These are the clients that generate the highest amounts of revenue to the firm, but because of their size they typically also take the most amount of work to close. Another potential downside for Large accounts is that they can also take a great deal of time to service and will often ask for increased services at lower rates. What percentage of your total revenue do you want to come from Large accounts in a given month, quarter, or year?

We have seen some firms rely on too much revenue coming from one or two Large accounts. As a result, they have suffered major setbacks after losing one (or both!) of them. We have also seen firms come close to going out of business because they were servicing too many Small accounts – clients who were taking up all of their time, but not generating enough revenue for the firm to be profitable. The key is to find the right mix of Small, Mid-Sized, and Large accounts for your business and your own career.

Revenue and Employees

Another way to look at client size is the actual size in terms of revenue and number of employees. By this standard, you will find that it may not make sense for you to spend time and money to prospect for Small and Mid-Sized clients. Your firm may have a history of success with one particular type of client, and it may make sense to continue to target that type of client. Or you may be looking to raise the bar on the types of companies you are targeting so that you can break into larger markets, and that might require different prospecting methods to get in front of those clients. The key is to have a plan, stick to that plan for a period of time, then track the results. If you are properly working the plan, and the results are not what you had hoped for, you can change or fine-tune the plan.

CREATE A PLAN→ TRACK THE PLAN → ADJUST THE PLAN

Firms tend to get into trouble when they do not track the success of their prospecting plan — and then they realize too late that their current plan is not working.

CASE IN POINT

A law firm we worked with was desperate to land a certain major energy company as a client, but was making no headway. It is typical for this type of company to use only three pre-approved legal vendors. We suggested that the law firm offer to come in for a day, for free, and advise the various departments individually on adherence to the new healthcare laws.

Once our client did that, the company asked their own vendors to do the same thing, so they would not have to use someone new. All of the company's current firms refused to provide a free, one-day compliance audit. Our client, by contrast, did provide the free one-day program — and the company was so happy with the job they did that our client landed on the approved vendor list.

As a result, the law firm ended up receiving a great deal of business from this company! This is an example of making appropriate adjustments to a prospecting plan. It is likely that our client never would have made this offer if we hadn't suggested it during a coaching session.

WHAT DO YOU DO BEST — AND FOR WHOM?

Especially if you are a solo or small firm, it is likely that you have already found and begun to focus on some special niche in the marketplace. What is it? Where is your expertise? What type of work do you prefer to do? What type of work is most profitable?

The biggest mistake you can make is to try to be a "jack of all trades and a master of none." Take an inventory of your strengths and weaknesses. Every professional has different strengths and weaknesses, and to be successful you need to take stock of where you and your firm can excel. Set goals and determine what will define success for you and your firm. Put your goals in writing and review them on a regular basis. Ideally, you should share your goals with a mentor, partner, or coach.

Who is the greatest golfer of this generation? If you answered Tiger Woods, we would agree. Does Tiger Woods have a coach? Absolutely! If he needs a coach, perhaps you do, too. Business development is a skill that needs to be developed over time. There are systems and processes to learn, strengths to be leveraged, weaknesses to be compensated for or overcome, and skills to practice. If you do not invest time with a coach addressing these issues, you are going to be at a great disadvantage in the marketplace. But with a coach, and a plan, and a little persistence, you can be successful in building up your book of business.

In the next chapter, we will discuss the efficient management of your time and financial resources.

Finding a mentor, marketing consultant, or business development coach will help you accelerate the process of creating your list of targets, developing action plans, tracking those plans, and making appropriate adjustments.

Recap: Three Kinds of Clients

- **Large** – these accounts generate the largest amount of revenue to the firm, but because of their size they typically take the most amount of work to close the business.
- **Mid-Sized** – these are accounts that fall in the middle range. In addition to revenue, you may want to look at the profitability of your client work when identifying this kind of account.
- **Small** – these are low-end clients (in terms of profitability and revenue). You must determine the number of such accounts that you can service, as well as the minimum amount of revenue a client could give you that would still make it worth your time to take on that new client.

CHAPTER SEVEN

Managing Your Time and Your Financial Resources

"If something works, it makes sense to do more of it, right?"

S ome professionals, as we have indicated, had no prospecting plan at all. Others make the effort to set up a plan, but do not take into account important everyday realities when they develop and refine the plan. They may have many fascinating business development ideas, but they do not stop to think about the practicality of their plan.

MORE ≠ BETTER

Ramping up whatever you are doing now, or thinking of doing now, may not always yield the best plan.

> **CASE IN POINT**
>
> The leadership of a technical consulting firm was looking to grow the practice in the pharmaceutical, healthcare, and biotechnical fields. The firm had had some success with advertising the previous year, so the owners

decided that they wanted to triple the amount of ads that they were going to place in technical journals over the next year. They had attended a conference in Las Vegas the previous year. At that conference, they had identified four additional conferences that they could attend. Two of these, it turned out, were conferences where they could exhibit in the coming year.

We asked the consultants if they had thought about the resources that would be needed to execute this plan. They admitted that they had not given it much thought, and really had not calculated the cost of exhibiting at the conferences and the advertising that they would place in the magazines and journals. As we began to ask additional questions regarding the cost of having their ads produced, the cost of materials for the displays to exhibit, the cost of travel and related conference expenses, and the cost of having several of their consultants out in the field for one week per conference, they quickly realized that their prospecting plan for the year simply did not make sense. They could not commit the amount of resources they had planned on investing.

TIME IS MONEY

One of the most important factors to consider when putting your prospecting plan together is the amount of time you can realistically dedicate to business development. We find that your profession, the time of year, your level of experience, and your role within your organization are all contributing factors to determining this. Some professionals, such as attorneys and accountants, might only have three to five hours per week to devote to business development because they are spending most of their time working on client matters. Some consultants and other professionals, by contrast, may have 50-75 percent of their time dedicated to business development, because others within the organization are completing the work.

When you put together your individual prospecting plan, or work with a coach to help you develop and refine that plan, be sure to identify just how much time you can and will dedicate to your business development role.

Some attorneys and accountants are able to dedicate, say, 30 focused minutes a day to business development, but only on days when they have relatively free schedules and are working in their own office. In that time, they might ask for referrals, call strategic partners, or follow up on new opportunities. During the weeks that these professionals are busy or at client sites, it's likely that no business development activity at all will take place for four days out of the week, but they might go to a networking event or have lunch with a strategic partner for two or three hours on the fifth day of that week. In such situations, we suggest a monthly, rather than a weekly, time target.

The key to successfully planning your business development time is to schedule out the blocks of time on your calendar, even if you are not quite sure what the activity will be. Our most successful clients do this to ensure that they reserve the appropriate amount of time to develop new business. Once you have a handle on the time slots you are dedicating to business development, you can then plan the activities that make the most sense for you based on your resources.

We often find that engineering firms and architectural firms will run into a major challenge when it comes to dedicating the time for business development. Our experience is that when these firms get busy with larger projects, all the business development activity gets pushed to the back burner. The firm will be profoundly busy for several months while the project is ongoing, and then people will realize that they are in deep trouble because there are no new opportunities in the pipeline after the big project ends. Why? No one has allocated any time to prospecting for new projects! For many firms, this means rollercoaster results, unpredictable revenues, and needless periods of stress over the course of the year.

> In order to have sustainable success, plan to participate in some kind of business development activity, even when you are very busy.

MONEY IS MONEY

The next step in creating your plan is to look at the financial resources you can invest for your business development plan.

Most service professionals do not have the resources necessary to advertise on television during the Super Bowl or the Academy Awards. By the same token, there are dozens of publications where you *could* advertise, and hundreds of professional associations that you *could* join, but it is simply not practical to spend money on every publication and join every group. Budgeting is all about setting priorities. Each year, you and your organization should create a budget for prospecting, and then allocate those funds in a way that is consistent with your plan. Set an expectation about the kind of return you expect for the dollars you are setting aside for your marketing and business development endeavors. Avoid the "expense account gone wild" syndrome!

CASE IN POINT

Many years ago, Joe, the managing partner of a mid-sized law firm, was attending one of our seminars. When we began discussing the topic of budgeting for business development, it looked as though smoke was coming out of Joe's ears!

As the conversation continued, we could see Joe was getting angrier and angrier. When we finally called on Joe, he could barely contain his rage. Joe's firm was spending money every year on expensive "club box tickets" to watch the local baseball team and the local football team. Joe said that he was spending tens of thousands of dollars per year on these events, and he was not realizing any return on his investment. He said that the professionals from his firm were quite happy to use the tickets, but he could not track a single new client that had materialized from this expense. In addition, Joe said that his firm was spending lots of money on dinners and "happy hours" that were not translating into any new business.

Later, we sat down with Joe to look more closely at what he was spending in marketing and business development dollars, in comparison with the return the firm was getting from the investment. We could see why Joe was so agitated. The firm was spending three times the national average on marketing and entertainment, and Joe had absolutely nothing to show for it! Over the next few weeks, we helped him to do some strategic planning, which resulted in Joe drastically changing his marketing plan and entertainment budget for the year.

Over the next year, Joe spent one-third of the money he was previously spending on entertainment, and his firm increased overall revenues by 35 percent. Thanks to some sound strategic planning, Joe's firm spent less money for a larger return. That is what working with a coach can accomplish!

In chapter fifteen of this book, you will find suggestions on the best ways to measure Return on Investment (ROI) for all of your business development activities. Once you are able to track the numbers, you can begin to have a more predictable business development plan.

In the next chapter, we will talk about where to look for prospective clients.

Recap: Business Development To-Do List

- Determine the amount of time per week that you can realistically dedicate to business development.
- Schedule the time on your calendar.
- Look critically at all the financial resources you invest for your business development plan.

CHAPTER EIGHT

Where Do I Find Prospective Clients?

"Where are the prospects, and how do I get them to listen to me?"

Now that we have discussed setting SMART goals for business development, developing targets, and looking at our time and financial resources for prospecting, it is time to identify some specific prospecting activities you can incorporate to meet your ideal prospect. In this chapter, we will introduce a wide variety of prospecting activities that have been successful for our clients over the years. You will find here a wide range of ideas, and it will be up to you to incorporate the ideas that will work best for you and your business.

STUDY YOUR HISTORY

If you have been involved with developing business in the past, the best place to start when investigating the effectiveness of your prospecting activities is to track which of those past activities have actually led to business. If certain prospecting activities have historically led to profitable business, you need to determine whether you can participate in more of those types of activities. If there are prospecting or marketing methods that have not worked in the past, it may be time to look for some other outlets for your activity.

DIVERSIFY

Incorporate between three and five *different* business development activities into your plan. If you become too reliant on one type of prospecting activity, that heavy focus on a single tactic can jeopardize your book of business, should that activity stop delivering positive results.

CASE IN POINT

Years ago, Sylvia, the principal of a consulting firm, came to us in a panic. Her firm had thrived for years on inbound leads they were receiving from their Web site and on leads from a targeted mailing campaign. Within one quarter, the leads they were receiving from each source had been cut by two-thirds, and their new business pipeline was getting smaller and smaller. The firm had not developed any additional ways to bring in business, and they were not sure how they were going to survive the year. Sylvia had over-relied on two lead sources she imagined would never run dry.

KEEP YOUR FRIENDS CLOSE

We place prospecting activities into different categories. The first major category of prospecting is all about what happens when you are prospecting utilizing current relationships.

Prospecting by utilizing current relationships can be very effective because the closing percentage tends to be much higher when you are referred into a new opportunity by someone you know, rather than trying to cold call to find an opportunity. Some activities that fall into this category include asking clients for referrals (which we will cover in chapter twelve), cross-selling and up-selling current clients (chapter nine), and leveraging your contacts (chapter eleven).

Most professionals do not realize how rich a potential source of business opportunities their own personal network is. One of the first exercises we ask our new clients to complete involves the creation of a list of people they already know well and can reach out to for referrals. Often, this one exercise will lead to new business for our clients within the first 30 days of our working together!

Unfortunately, most people cannot rely strictly on their current relationships to hit their new business goals. The reason is that many of the clients whom you want to target probably lie outside of your current circle of relationships. It may be time to move beyond your comfort zone by identifying some different methods of prospecting — methods that target key accounts or types of prospects that you have identified and cannot reach by means of your personal network.

INTRODUCING YOURSELF IS HALF THE BATTLE

The next big category of prospecting activities includes those activities that allow you to physically meet new potential clients.

This brings us to the "Three Foot Rule," a Sandler rule that states that anyone within three feet of you is either a prospect or is someone who might be able to refer you to a prospect. Initiate conversations with such people! You do not have to go to a special event to follow this rule. It can apply to people you meet in the course of your everyday activities. Most professionals have children or grandchildren who participate in sports, recitals, and similar school-related activities. How often do you go to events where other grownups are just standing around?

No, we do not want you to "sell" those other parents — but you might want to ask them what they do for a living when they are not attending their kids' activities. Typically, as they talk about what they do, they will talk about their job. After you ask some intelligent questions about them, they will almost always ask what *you* do for a living. Whenever you hear that question, we will suggest you answer with your 30-second commercial (crafting that important message is covered in chapter ten).

If the person with whom you are speaking seems interested, suggest that you exchange phone numbers and talk business *during business hours* — not while you are both involved in family-centered activities!

CASE IN POINT

Molly is a pharmacist. She sits on the fundraising board of her daughter's school. One day, as she was speaking with one of the parents of another child, she learned that parent was a director at a local nursing home — exactly the type of prospect Molly was looking to target. One week later, at the other parent's suggestion, they had a meeting scheduled to speak over coffee. A business relationship followed!

However, the Three Foot Rule does not only apply exclusively to events involving your children!

CASE IN POINT

Bob is an attorney who played on a weekly men's ice hockey team. Bob had played on the same team for four years, and when we asked him what the other people on his team did for a living, Bob told us that he was not sure.

We asked Bob how many people on his team knew that he was an attorney, and Bob was pretty sure that most of his teammates did not know that. At our suggestion, Bob began a weekly routine of asking one person on the team to meet him for coffee before the game. At the meetings, Bob simply asked the other person about what he did for a living, and about halfway into the conversation, Bob's teammate would ask him the same thing. Over the next three months, Bob received five new clients from his teammates!

NETWORK

Networking is another way for you to meet with people who are currently outside your sphere of influence.

Depending on your marketplace and the scope of your work, you could join industry associations (many of our legal clients join their local Bar Association because a good number of referrals for attorneys come from other attorneys), professional associations where your clients or potential clients are members, local chambers of commerce, or lead swap/networking groups. The key to networking is to find one or two groups whose membership comprises the types of industries and organizations that you would like to target.

In addition, we suggest that you get involved with industry groups, and volunteer to take on leadership positions at such groups, so that you can make a contribution — and begin to develop relationships with the people you meet within these organizations.

CASE IN POINT

One of our clients is an architect named Paul. He was known as a "master networker" because he knew about all of the different events related to his industry, and he was attending almost every event. Paul had a challenge, though: he was seeing the same people over and over again, and not meeting any of the decision makers he needed to meet to win new projects.

At our suggestion, Paul took over a sub-group in one of the associations to which he belonged, and took on the goal of acquiring high-profile speakers for monthly events. Paul began to call on people who might not have taken his call if they knew he was trying to solicit them for their business, but were certainly interested in speaking to a group of professionals.

Paul used this role to schedule face-to-face meetings, and several of these meetings developed into new opportunities for him.

All Networks Are Not Created Equal

If you do decide to join professional groups and add this kind of networking to your prospecting arsenal, make sure that you track the time and money you are spending with these organizations, as well as the amount of new business and referrals that you are generating from your membership. It is important to measure the return on investment from these activities! Ideally, you should be tracking this on a quarterly basis. If you find that you are spending time and money on an activity or group that is not leading to new business, start to look for a more productive group that will give you a stronger return.

ARCTIC EXPLORATION

The last major category that your prospecting activity may fall into is what we define as "cold prospecting." Cold prospecting is reaching out to people you do not know or with whom you have no mutual connection.

Years ago, cold calling was the primary way that people would reach out to prospects. Even today, it might make sense for some professionals to cold call, but for others this form of contact is impractical and may even violate their profession's code of ethics.

Today, social media (which we cover in chapter thirteen) is one way to reach out to people whom you do not know. Another way to try to reach new prospects is through facilitating workshops and seminars (chapter fourteen). You will also want to consider investing in a good professional Web site and utilizing Search Engine Optimization (SEO), as these investments can help to drive new traffic to your site. An additional way to reach new prospects is through newsletters (mailed or electronic), blogs, LinkedIn® posts, and podcasts.

Cold prospecting will not lead to as high a closing percentage as utilizing current relationships (see the chart below), but it may help you to penetrate markets where you do not currently have a presence. The estimates below are based on the reports that we receive from our clients in the field.

Category of Prospecting   **Expected Closing %**

Cold Calls   **Under 1 %**
(You do not know the person, just the name of the organization.)

Cool Call   **Under 5 %**
(You know the name of the organization and the person you are trying to reach, but that person does not know who you are.)

Lead   **25-30 %**
(You have the name of the person who made the recommendation or a joint email has been sent out, but nobody has talked to that person about you.)

Referral   **50 %**
(The person you are calling knows who you are, why you are calling, and has agreed to take your call.)

Personal Introduction   **85 %**
(The person referring you is coming with you to provide a personal introduction.)

There are over 20 different prospecting activities you can utilize to develop relationships with potential clients. The key for success in business development is to mix and match the different prospecting methods that are appropriate for your target marketplace, and then track the success of each marketing activity.

As we have said, you will want to implement a mix of three to five different prospecting activities. These activities could range from utilizing your current relationships to trying some of the colder prospecting activities with the aim of increasing your exposure to a larger number of potential clients.

In addition, we would suggest that you take a communications-style assessment and a behavioral assessment to determine your natural strengths and weaknesses when it comes to business development. These assessments will afford you an edge by showing you which prospecting activities will give you the greatest chance of success based on those strengths and weaknesses. Finally, to maximize success, remember that you should be working with a coach who will help you to evaluate the results of these assessments, track your results, and hold you accountable for engaging in the activities you commit to in your plan.

In the next chapter, we will talk about developing additional business by leveraging the clients you already have.

Recap: Three Categories of Prospecting

- **Current Relationships** – Prospecting by utilizing your relationships can be very effective because the closing percentage is much higher when you are referred into a new opportunity rather than trying to cold call to find an opportunity.
- **Physical Contact** – Those activities that allow you to physically meet potential clients, including social functions, hobbies, industry associations, etc.
- **Cold Prospecting** – Reaching out to people you do not know.

CHAPTER NINE

Up-Selling and Cross-Selling

*"My clients respect me and the work I do. I do not want
to diminish that by pushing them to buy more."*

The most time- and cost-effective way to develop more business
is to provide more services to your current clients.

The formal definition of cross-selling is "the action or practice
of selling among or between clients, markets, traders, etc. or the action
or practice of selling an additional product or service to an existing
client." In essence, cross-selling means providing additional services in
new areas or departments for your current client base. Many professionals provide a wide variety of services, and the quickest way for them to
grow their revenues is to uncover additional opportunities with a client
who is already familiar with their work.

THE "FIELD OF DREAMS" FALLACY

Do you remember the movie "Field of Dreams"? The film's most famous
line was, "If you build it, they will come." When it comes to selling professional services, the motto should be: "If you build it, they *might* come
— but first, they have to know that it exists!"

When we discuss cross-selling with professionals, many of them tell us that they are uncomfortable with the concept. Many professionals find that cross-selling is outside of their comfort zone, and when we suggest that professionals start cross-selling within their current client base, we are likely to hear a variety of excuses about why they will not or cannot cross-sell. Some of the most common excuses are: "I do not want to seem like I am begging for business," or "My clients know to come to me if they need my firm's services," or "I do not want to come across as 'salesy.'" Other professionals will share with us that they are uncomfortable with cross-selling because they either do not trust their partners to provide good work for their clients, or they simply forget to ask.

Our experience is that *all* of these self-limiting beliefs are our own creation, and are typically not shared by our clients.

THE BENEFITS OF ONE-STOP SHOPPING

In our discussions with clients across multiple disciplines, the feedback that we receive is that many companies would prefer to receive multiple services from one provider.

Clients tell us that they enjoy working with a single provider because they then have one firm with an understanding of everything that is happening, rather than the services being provided in silos and nobody having a handle on "the big picture."

Clients also say that another benefit of utilizing one firm for multiple services is that they can better keep costs under control and track their spending more easily, which typically translates into an overall cost savings.

In addition, if something goes wrong, a client has one source to address for an answer, rather than having multiple providers blame each other for problems that arise.

CROSS-SELLING — STEP-BY-STEP

Clients often ask us: "How do we cross-sell without looking like we just want to sell our clients additional services and bill more?" We suggest that you take the following steps if your aim is to cross-sell in a professional manner.

1. Make Sure They Are Happy

Begin with this principle: *They will not spend more if they are not happy with what they have!*

First and foremost, you must make sure that your client is satisfied with the services that you are currently providing. We suggest you schedule a time to have a check-in conversation with your client. Encourage your client to share any issues or concerns he may have with your services. If your client mentions an issue or service that he is unhappy with, forget the cross-selling conversation and focus on correcting the problems.

Some people are uncomfortable having this conversation because they are afraid of the feedback they might receive. Reality check: If a client has negative feedback, it is much better to receive the negative feedback while that person is still a client — and you still have a chance to fix the problem. This is far preferable to hearing about the problems someone had with your services after the client has decided to work with someone else!

2. Ask for Permission

Once you have confirmed that your client is happy with your services, ask your client's permission to ask a question. We find that once people give you permission to do something, like ask a question, they do not get upset when you actually do. In addition, if you are uncomfortable having the conversation, you should share with your client that you are uncomfortable.

3. Make Your Case

Once you have received permission to ask the question (which you will pose in step four, below), share with your client that there are multiple services you provide for clients above and beyond the work you are currently providing for them, and you would like to make them aware of what those services entail. Some of our clients will use an extended 30-second commercial — covered in chapter ten — to discuss additional problems they can solve for their clients. Other professionals will share extended examples that demonstrate how other clients have benefited by using more than just one of their services.

4. "Does This Make Sense for You?"

After you discuss the different services you have provided for other clients, ask the person you are speaking with if he has any of the same issues that you have helped other clients solve. If your client tells you your other services do not make sense for him, or if he is happy with the other providers that he is working with, you can simply tell him that you appreciate that he took the time to listen.

5. Taking the Next Step

If the people you are talking to are interested in other services that you provide, ask them what they believe the next steps should be for you to have that conversation. If it makes sense for you to include someone else from your firm or their company in the conversation, set up a way to facilitate a warm introduction to the client contact.

CASE IN POINT

Alan is the managing partner of a law firm that practiced eight different areas of business law. When we first spoke with Alan, he was considering closing the employment law practice of the firm because that practice area was not profitable. We suggested to Alan that he delay his decision to close that practice area. We told Alan that if the partners in the law firm were willing to cross-sell and focus on the employment practice, we could help Alan make that practice group profitable for his firm.

When we asked Alan about the cross-selling practices of the firm (there were over 400 attorneys in the firm), he was unsure whether any partners were proactively cross-selling. At our suggestion, Alan required every partner with a client employing 25 or more employees to refer at least one of these clients to someone in the employment practice area. In twelve months, the firm generated over $1,000,000 in new business for the employment group — all from its current clients!

MISSED OPPORTUNITY

When a firm does a poor job at cross-selling, that carries far-reaching consequences. Consider the following true story.

CASE IN POINT

Susan works in a small engineering firm that provides both civil engineering services and environmental consulting services. Susan was meeting with a good client of hers, and during the conversation Susan's client happened to mention that he was very unhappy with the environmental work he had just received from one of Susan's competitors.

When Susan asked why her client was using a different firm for environmental work, her client said that he did not even realize her firm provided environmental work ... but, since he was thrilled with the civil engineering services he was getting, he would be happy to give them the environmental work! When Susan asked how often environmental work came up for the client, she learned that it arose four to six times per year. Susan had been working with this client for over five years. When she realized the amount of revenue she had missed out on, she wished she had taken action earlier.

UP-SELLING

Up-selling is providing additional or "add-on" services for a client for whom you are already providing work.

CASE IN POINT

Larry owns an IT consulting firm that provides customized software solutions; his main clients are hospitals and healthcare organizations. Larry noticed that when he was working with his clients, projects would become stalled because the client's internal IT staff was so busy working on essential services for the healthcare organization that they did not have time to work on external projects.

When Larry brought this to our attention in a coaching session, we asked him if he had the capability to augment the staff of the organizations with which he worked. Larry said that he could indeed provide those services, and when he called his clients, he learned that they were thrilled to have the opportunity to hire experts who could help them complete these specialized projects.

Over the next six months, Larry's business model changed from a software company to a software and services company. Larry increased his business by 40 percent simply by up-selling current clients. Once Larry proved that he was able to provide good staff support to his clients, he was able to cross-sell into different departments within those clients, which led to additional business.

Larry now has more revenue coming from the services and staffing side of his business than he does from the software side of his business.

CROSS-SELLING OR UP-SELLING: THE SAME RULES APPLY

The process of up-selling is very similar to the process of cross-selling. First, it is important to make sure that your client is happy with the services you are currently providing. Next, ask your client if it is OK to ask a question and have a conversation about additional services your organization provides to its clients. After you get permission, use a 30-second commercial (you'll learn about this in the next chapter) or tell third-party stories about the ways other clients utilize all of your different services. Finally, ask if it makes sense to have a further discussion about whether those additional services make sense for your client.

> Cross-selling and up-selling are easy ways to develop more business from your current clients. Because you have already developed a relationship with them, you will find that your clients are more receptive to your services than someone with whom you are speaking for the first time.

Most professionals find that when they implement cross-selling and up-selling, the amount of time to close a new opportunity shortens. Because they are now providing multiple services to their clients, they tend to work with their clients for a longer period of time.

In the next chapter, you will learn how to develop a powerful 30-second commercial.

> **Recap:** The most time- and cost-effective way to develop more business is to provide more services to your current clients, either through cross-selling or up-selling.
>
> - Make sure they are happy with the services you are providing.
> - Ask for permission to ask a question.
> - Make your case.
> - Ask, "Does this make sense to you?"

CHAPTER TEN

Developing a 30-Second Commercial that Differentiates You from the Competition

"Why not just tell them when we were founded?"

Over the course of your career, you will probably attend more networking events, seminars, conferences, trade shows, and happy hours than you can count. If you are like most of the professionals we have met, you have not given much thought ahead of time to the question of how you will introduce yourself when meeting someone at these events for the first time.

If someone were to walk up to you right now and ask you what you did for a living, what would you say?

Would you begin by talking about when your firm or practice was founded, or about how you chose your particular career path, or what your personal area of expertise is?

How do *you* react when someone begins sharing that kind of information at an event? Does it leave you enthralled? Or does it make you look around the room for someone else who is a better conversationalist?

Here is the real question: how much time and energy have you devoted to *preparing* your elevator pitch or 30-second commercial?

> If you are not prepared to deliver a truly powerful 30-second commercial, you may miss out on your chance to convert a conversation with someone into a new client opportunity.

We find that most of the clients we have worked with have many competitors in their marketplace, and one of the biggest challenges they face is the need to differentiate themselves from the competition. If you are not able to differentiate yourself from your competitors within the first 30 seconds of an initial conversation, you will not be able to convert that conversation into a new business opportunity. That is a lost opportunity.

How Not To Make a Good First Impression

Try this exercise. Remember back to the last event that you attended when you were meeting new people for the first time. Think about the other professionals that you met at this event. How did *they* introduce themselves? If you cannot remember, pay close attention to how your peers introduce themselves at the next event you attend.

In general, we find that when most professionals introduce themselves, they talk about the features and benefits of working with them and their firms. They mention attributes such as the size of their firm or company, specialty, location, and services. Most describe themselves as experts in a particular field. They talk about the fact that they are service oriented, and about their ability to deliver good results.

The messages they send are typically very "I-centered." These messages are all about the person or enterprise delivering the message, and *not* about the person to whom they are speaking. Think about that for a moment. What does that kind of messaging sound like to your audience?

"I offer expertise in blah blah blah..." "We offer affordable yada yada yada..." "We are proud of our record of service to hummanah hummanah hummanah..."

Here is another question: Have you ever heard these people say that they *weren't* an expert, that they *overcharged* their clients, or that they provided *poor* service? You have probably never heard those things. That would be a memorable 30-second commercial for all the wrong reasons!

So what kind of answer are *you* likely to give when someone asks, "What do you do?" Are you planning to do what everyone does, which is "wing it"? If you do, you will be talking about yourself and your own company, just as everyone else does. Again: Notice that the vast majority of these introductions are I-focused, and are *not* focused on the potential issues that could arise for their clients. If you decide to lump your message in with all the other messages that sound like that — you have a problem!

Does This Sound Familiar?

A typical commercial heard at a networking event might sound like this:

> "My name is Joe Smith, and I am with the XYZ accounting firm. We are a full service firm located in Anywhere, USA. We provide tax services, audit services, and forensic accounting, and we have over 100 professionals in our firm. We provide great service for our clients, and we give them good value for what they pay us. I'd like to talk to you about how we can help you."

Are you wondering how we knew what you said at these events?

Even worse, are you still wondering what is wrong with that commercial?

The question we would ask is, if there are five other similar firms at this networking event, would the person with this particular commercial stand out?

Many professionals are too broad in describing their services. We have spoken with many attorneys who introduce themselves at an event, and then find that the person with whom they are speaking will start asking about, say, wills — when the attorney's specialty is in, say, intellectual property or litigation! This is a sign that they need to prepare their 30-second commercial more carefully. Somehow, they need to learn to introduce themselves within 30 seconds or less in a way that will identify the *problems* they can help their clients solve — without getting too specific.

The Next Five Minutes

We have already spoken about the importance of being perceived as a strategic advisor rather than as a vendor. The 30-second commercial is the first tool you will use to shape this perception in your favor.

When you introduce yourself, your goal is to make a positive impact that elicits interest. The reaction you want to generate from the person with whom you are speaking is simply for them to want to continue the conversation with you.

Most professionals are selling complicated services and could never realistically sign up a new client within the initial 30 seconds of meeting someone. That is one of the main reasons that we do not want to "sell" with the 30-second commercial.

> The goal of the 30-second commercial is simply to get the person you are in front of to want to speak with you for an additional five minutes.

The analogy we like to use for the 30-second commercial is that of a resume. On its own, a resume is never going to get someone a job. The purpose of the resume is to intrigue your audience enough to bring you in for an interview!

Similarly, the 30-second commercial should get your audience interested enough to keep listening for the next few minutes. That is *all* you want it to do. We suggest to our clients that they should look, sound, and feel different from all of their competitors at all times. You do not want to appear as if you are selling something; you want to be perceived as an expert. The 30-second commercial is the technique that will allow you to accomplish those goals in the very early stages of the conversation.

> Standing out from your competitors begins with leaving an outstanding first impression.

Think of yourself as what you are: a problem-solver. It is likely that some potential clients you meet while at an event have issues you are good at resolving, issues that need to be resolved sooner rather than later. When you utilize a well-crafted, effective 30-second commercial, you immediately present yourself as a problem-solver and advisor who is relevant to that listener's world. The 30-second commercial is designed to engage someone in conversation, and to gauge whether or not he has, or he knows someone else who may have, the types of problems or concerns that you can solve.

IDENTIFYING THE PROBLEM

The best way to begin developing your 30-second commercial is to think about the specific problems that you solve for your clients.

What are the challenges your potential clients might encounter? What types of issues could cost them money, opportunities, or open them up to liability? Are your prospects spending a great deal of their time on issues or projects that you could handle, thereby freeing up their time and allowing them to focus on other, more essential issues?

We suggest that when starting a conversation with people at a networking event or social gathering, you ask them to tell you a little about themselves first. Getting the other person to speak first accomplishes several goals. First, it makes the person with whom you are speaking a lot more comfortable because people like to talk about themselves more than they like to talk about anything else. Second, as they talk about themselves, you can learn a little more about their background, and this will help you to customize your message when you deliver your 30-second commercial.

When discussing the problems that you solve for your potential clients, begin by talking about the big picture problems that you solve. You want to tap into the emotional part of their brain as you do this. We suggest that you utilize emotional words such as frustrated, upset, or disappointed when discussing the problems you can help your clients to overcome because these are powerful emotions that are likely to connect to existing problems you can solve.

In addition, you may want to utilize case studies and third-party stories. The more vivid the story, the more your prospects can see themselves experiencing the same issues.

At the end of your commercial, it is important to ask an open-ended question. You want to get the person with whom you are speaking to self-identify which of the issues that you have mentioned are most relevant.

There is no one right way to do this. To the contrary, there are many different ways to craft a powerful 30-second commercial.

Here is one example of an effective 30-second commercial.

"My name is Evan; I'm with Sandler Training. I work with professionals who, despite their previous successes and current best efforts, are not growing their firms as quickly and consistently as they would like. By helping them restructure and refocus their business development efforts around a few select activities, they're able to identify and develop new business opportunities more quickly and generate referrals more consistently — even if they have limited time to devote to the effort or are uncomfortable stepping into a selling role. How comfortable are you with the results of your business growth efforts?"

Here's another example:

"My name is Evan and I am with Sandler Training. We work with professionals who, despite their best efforts, are frustrated because they just are not developing as much new business as they would like. Some are upset because they spend so much time servicing their clients that they just do not know how they are going to be able to put together a business development plan, make the time to execute that plan and bring in as many new opportunities as they would like. Others are concerned because the tactics and strategies that worked in the past to develop new business are just not working anymore. Others do great work for their clients and are concerned because they are not getting as many referrals as they know they should. Finally, many people are getting squeezed regarding their rates. Which of those issues are you facing?"

A (LITERAL) ELEVATOR PITCH

A good 30-second commercial can be deployed at any appropriate place and time — including the opportunity that arises for a classic "elevator pitch."

CASE IN POINT

Walter is an attorney. One day, Walter was walking into a large office building when a young woman stepped into the elevator with him. Walter had been working with us for a while and was a naturally friendly person, so he asked the woman what she did for a living. The woman told him she was in real estate and that her company worked on commercial deals. She then asked Walter what he did for a living. Walter shared a powerful 30-second commercial, structurally very similar to what you just read, and mentioned that he was an attorney who helped real estate firms who were frustrated/upset/concerned about various problems he had a demonstrated track record of solving.

The woman told Walter that her company was looking for someone with precisely his experience, and she asked if he would come to her office to meet her boss. Walter walked into the real estate firm's office, and 45 minutes later he walked out with a new client.

Imagine what Walter would have missed if he had not started that conversation ... or if he would have responded with a typical "I-focused" message!

Below is a worksheet you can use to help you put together your initial 30-second commercial. If you are still unclear about what frustrates, upsets, and concerns your best clients, you will want to pay special attention to chapter nineteen, which talks in even more depth about the important topic of pain. For now, consider that the consequences of the *absence* of the features and benefits you provide equals pain.

30 Second Pain-Provoking Commercial Worksheet

Features/Benefits of your Firm's Service(s)	Consequences of Not Having this Feature/Benefit = PAIN

My name is _____ with _____(company/firm).
We are a _____ (two to four word descriptor of your company or firm) and help clients/businesses who are concerned about:

(PAIN 1) _____, (PAIN 2) _____, (PAIN 3) _____.

Which of these things should we discuss? OR
Which of those challenges have you faced?

DIFFERENT COMMERCIALS FOR DIFFERENT AUDIENCES

The key to creating a successful 30-second commercial is to understand that you must create different commercials for different audiences.

If you are an attorney, accountant, or consultant with multiple practice areas in your firm, you should create a commercial for your specific practice area, as well as a firm-wide commercial touching on other practice areas.

CASE IN POINT

One of our clients, Mike, is a litigation attorney with a large law firm. Mike was frustrated because he would attend several networking events per month but never found new business opportunities. As we provided coaching for Mike, we asked him to recite the introduction that he used at the events. His introduction briefly mentioned his firm, and then he went into (boring) detail about how he handled litigation for his clients. In other words, he did not stand out.

Once he was done with his commercial, we asked Mike how often he met someone who either had just been sued or was about to be sued by someone. He admitted that it was not an everyday occurrence to meet someone who had an immediate need for a litigator. We then asked Mike how many practice areas existed within his (large) firm. He counted eight different business practice areas. We went on to ask if he ever received origination credit if he brought work into the firm that was completed by attorneys in different practice areas. He told us that he did get credit for business that was completed outside of his department if he originated the work.

We helped Mike build a general, firm-wide 30-second commercial addressing big picture problems that business owners were likely to face, such as:

- Believing they were not getting value for the fees they were paying their current attorney.
- Feeling frustrated because they were using two or three different small specialty firms to handle their matters, which was costing them more money.
- Feeling upset that the attorneys from different firms did not coordinate their efforts to come up with a business-wide strategy for the company.

Over the next six months, Mike developed $250,000 in new business by using his firm-wide commercial when meeting new people. All of this was new business that he developed for practice areas outside of litigation!

It gets better. Two of those clients ran into issues where they needed litigation over the next eighteen months. That resulted in an additional $150,000 of work for which Mike was awarded credit.

Not Just for Clients

Many of our clients will also develop a 30-second commercial to present to potential referral partners and strategic partners. These commercials are not going to sound the same as the commercials you use with prospective clients!

Referral partners and strategic partners have different needs than your clients, so you need to make sure that you talk about the issues that are important to them. Some of those needs might be concern about how their clients and contacts are being serviced, frustration because their referral partners are not providing value or resources for the strategic partner, or disappointment with a lack of communication.

> The 30-second commercial is one of the most powerful tools you will learn about in this book, but it will also be one of the most uncomfortable for you to begin to use.

Beyond the Comfort Zone

Many of us have introduced ourselves in exactly the same way for the last 10, 20, 30 years or more. It will take practice and a conscious effort for you to move out of your comfort zone and begin introducing yourself in a different way. Most of our clients find that they need to practice their new commercial 50-100 times before they are comfortable talking about the problems they solve, rather than listing the services they provide.

Once you do become comfortable with your new 30-second commercial, you will find that more of your initial conversations will convert into new potential client opportunities.

In the next chapter, we will talk more about referrals and how to ask for them.

Recap: The 30-Second Commercial

- It is not about you!
- Do not sell anything. Generate interest for the next five minutes of conversation.
- Identify what initially frustrates/upsets/concerns clients you have helped.
- At the end of the commercial, ask an open-ended question.
- One size does not fit all! Create commercials for multiple audiences.

CHAPTER ELEVEN

Leveraging Your Contacts

"But wait! THEY should be calling ME, right?"

Business development requires prospecting, which means reaching out to people even though you might prefer that they call you. And when it comes to prospecting, it is better to work smart than to work hard.

One of the biggest mistakes professionals make when it comes to business development is not taking advantage of their biggest assets: their contacts and their relationships. In our experience, it is much quicker and much easier to develop business and find new relationships by working through the people you know and trust, rather than reaching out to people through cold calls or responding to requests for proposals and quotes.

ASKING IS NOT IMPOSING

One of the primary reasons people do not reach out and leverage their contacts is that doing so is outside of their comfort zone. When we ask our clients whether they have reached out to their relationships to try to generate new business, we hear excuses and self-limiting beliefs such as, "I do not want to be a bother," or "I do not want to come across as desperate for business." Sometimes we will also hear statements like, "I do not want to come across like a salesperson," "I do not want to be too pushy," or "People already know what I do, and if they can help me or know someone that I should meet, they will reach out to me."

When we hear those statements from our clients, we ask them if any of their friends, contacts, or clients have ever reached out to *them* to ask for help. Of course, our clients then tell us that they will occasionally get requests to help the people in their network. We then ask our clients if they ever feel as though a contact with whom they have a good relationship is "taking advantage" of them when they are asked for help.

Typically, the answer is that they *never* feel taken advantage of, and that they are happy to help their contacts whenever their contacts reach out to them. Our final question to our clients is: "Why do you think your clients or contacts will think you are desperate if you ask them for help?"

When we ask that question, it is usually followed by about ten seconds of silence. The client will then say that they never thought about things that way, and that people with whom they have good relationships probably would be willing to help them.

Who Will You Call?

Once you are able to move out of your comfort zone, and you feel comfortable with the idea of leveraging your clients and contacts to develop new relationships, the next step is to create a list of people you may be able to contact for help. There are several categories of people you might be able to reach out to for conversations about how they can help you.

Many of our clients have current and former clients who are happy with their work — and happy clients are a natural place to start in creating a list of people to reach out to for referrals and introductions. You may have strategic partners or referral partners who can provide complementary services to those your firm or company offers. Why not reach out to them for potential referrals and advice? Members of professional and trade associations where you have developed relationships can be another good source of help when looking for contacts to potentially leverage.

Another area where many people have maintained good relationships is with former classmates. Many of our clients have found great success in reconnecting with people through LinkedIn and their alumni associations. Other clients have maintained relationships with people at organizations where they have worked in the past, or with people who have left their organization.

LEARNING YOUR ABCs

Once you have developed a list of contacts and relationships, the next step is to divide that list into three categories. The first category is the "A" contact list. The criteria for your "A" contacts are people with whom you have a good relationship, and who would likely return your phone call or email within 48 hours. Your "A" contacts should also be well positioned to introduce you to the types of clients you would like to meet. When you look to schedule meetings to attempt to leverage your contacts, you should start with your "A" list. Most of our clients find that their "A" list is the smallest, but conversations with people on your "A" list generally provide you with the best warm contacts.

Your "B" list of contacts are those people who would return your phone call within one week. People on your "B" list may not have as many obvious connections to the people that you would like to meet. Once you have exhausted your list of "A" contacts, you should then begin to contact your "B" contacts.

The last category of contacts are your "C" list of contacts. Your "C" list of contacts are those people who do not fit into your "A" or "B" lists. These contacts may be people you have only met once or twice, people who are your acquaintances, or people with whom you are connected on LinkedIn, but you do not remember who they are or how they got connected to you. Many professionals who complete this exercise begin to realize that many of their contacts fall into this "C" list category. We suggest that you reach out to your "C" list contacts only after you have exhausted all of your "A" list and "B" list contacts.

Once you have identified a list of people to reach out to, it is time to start calling the people on your list.

CASE IN POINT

Mike is a business attorney with a mid-sized law firm, and one of the first actions that Mike took when we began working together was to create his list. Mike decided to make two calls per day to people on his "A" and "B" lists. Mike's "A" list consisted of current clients and family members who were in the business community. After the first week, Mike had scheduled four appointments with people in his network, and by the end of the first month, Mike received five referrals from the people who he had met. Mike also reported that the conversations were much easier than what he pictured in his mind, and that the people he had relationships with were happy that they could help him. Mike retained two new clients within the first 45 days of working with us strictly through leveraging his contacts.

In the next chapter, you will learn how to ask for referrals in a professional manner.

Recap: Leveraging Your Contact Base

Move out of your Comfort Zone, and you will begin to feel comfortable with the idea of leveraging your clients and contacts to develop new relationships.

- Create your list of "A," "B" and "C" contacts!
- Your "A" contacts are people with whom you have a good relationship, who would return your phone call or email within 48 hours, and who are well positioned to introduce you to the types of clients you would like to meet.
- Your "B" list of contacts are those people you know who would return your phone call within one week, and who may not have as many obvious connections to the people you would like to meet. Once you have exhausted your list of "A" contacts, you should begin to contact your "B" contacts.
- The last category of contacts are your "C" list of contacts — those contacts who do not fit into your "A" or "B" lists. These may be people you have only met once or twice, people who are your acquaintances, or people with whom you are connected on LinkedIn, but you do not remember who they are or how they got connected to you.

CHAPTER TWELVE

Ask for Referrals in a Professional Manner

"I worked hard for these relationships, and I am not going to ruin them by begging for phone numbers."

It is an interesting contradiction. The number one technique for generating more clients is also the technique that makes us the most uncomfortable.

Numerous studies have shown that the most effective way to develop more business is through referrals. Typically, referrals come from four sources: other professionals, strategic partners, current clients, and former clients.

Let us begin by exploring some of the limiting beliefs that professionals hold onto that keep them from asking for referrals.

WE ARE NOT AS IMPORTANT AS WE THINK WE ARE

Some professionals will not ask for referrals because they believe that others should already know that they are good at what they do, and should automatically give them their business when a need arises. It would be nice to be able to believe that our contacts are always thinking about us ... but that is almost never the case. Most people are constantly tuned into the same radio station, *WIIFM* ("What's In It For Me"). They do not spend their days and nights thinking about ways that they could help us.

Think about how busy *you* are in your day-to-day life, and think about how often *you* think of referrals you should pass along to others. That probably does not happen as often as it should. If you want to receive referrals, you will need to remind people that you are available, and you must be able to ask for the business. Not only that, but you will also need to teach your contacts how to give you a good referral.

Proactive Does Not Equal Desperate

Another reason people will not ask for referrals is the belief that others will think they are desperate if they ask for business. Most professionals have the self-limiting belief that their peers and clients will think less of them if they "ask for business."

Yet when professionals do ask for referrals, they are often surprised by how much their peers want to help them. Our clients are usually surprised at how easy it is to ask for referrals ... once they learn the most effective way to do it.

"Quid Pro Quo?"

Many professionals do not ask for referrals because they are afraid they have nothing to offer in return. They are often surprised when they discover that the referring party's only expectation is that their client or friends receive the best service. When you ask for referrals, the other party typically expects less in return than you would think.

CASE IN POINT

Karen is a wetlands scientist for a large engineering firm. For the first ten years of her career, her only role was to provide client service and work on projects. Karen's firm identified her as someone they wanted to train to develop business, so she entered our ongoing business development training program. Karen was very client-centered, and she was extremely concerned with coming across as too pushy or too needy to her clients. Initially, Karen was very uncomfortable with the thought of asking for referrals. She thought it would be too pushy, and she believed that others would not have the time to help her.

Eventually, Karen got sick of us asking her to ask for referrals. One day, she was on-site with one of her firm's largest clients. This client was a large government agency that was giving her firm some work, but not a lot. Karen asked the person with whom she was meeting if there was anyone else in the department she should meet.

Karen's contact proceeded to walk her around the office and introduce her to seven different people who were responsible for selecting engineers and wetlands scientists for new projects. In addition, that person sent emails to four additional people who were not in the office that day.

Karen developed over $250,000 in business over the next eighteen months from the people she was referred to that day!

STARTING SMALL

What will it take to overcome the fears or discomfort associated with asking for referrals? Our clients have found that they cannot overcome years of self-limiting beliefs regarding referrals in one or two weeks. They must constantly work on their behavior to overcome their fear of asking others for help.

We suggest that you begin in a low risk situation. Do not ask for a referral from your largest client the first time you decide to ask. Start with a long-term client who has a stake in your success, or with a friend or strategic partner. Do not put pressure on the person you approach. Let your client or referral partner know that it is OK if they cannot think of someone to refer to you. You do not want to jeopardize a relationship when you ask for a referral!

You can easily make the act of asking for referrals part of your strategy for retaining and growing your current clients just by beginning with a discussion about how the client perceives the quality of the work being delivered. This discussion will help you to determine whether you need to pay more attention to that client — or perhaps reinforce what a good job you are currently doing! In the latter case, it is easy to make the transition to asking for a referral.

Asking for referrals will also help you with time management. When your clients help you to hit your prospecting targets, that may free up time you can devote to servicing your clients!

Use the worksheet below to calculate what *not* asking for referrals is costing you.

How Much Money Have You Left on the Table?

1. Number of client meetings in the last month: _____

2. Potential number of referrals: _____
    (multiply line 1 by 3)

3. Actual number of referrals you got from those calls: _____

4. Number of referrals you left on the table: _____
    (subtract line 3 from line 2)

5. Number of potential clients you gave up: _____
    (multiply line 4 by 50%)

6. Revenue you did not take to the bank: _____
    (multiply line 5 by your average account value)

TEN TIPS FOR INCREASING REFERRALS

1. Ask for Referrals

Studies have shown that 20 percent of the people you know will automatically give you referrals, and another 20 percent are uncomfortable giving referrals and will never give them out. Your job is to ask the other 60 percent properly.

2. Understand Your Target Market

It is difficult for people to give you referrals if you cannot tell them the types of prospects you would like to meet. Make sure you know who your target market is, and relay this information to the people you approach for referrals.

3. Create a Target List

Make sure that you have a list of prospects you would like to do business with, and carry that list with you everywhere.

4. Do Not Accept a Lead Instead of a Referral

Many times our contacts will say, "Call John and just use my name when you call." Our experience tells us that these leads will only turn into business 25-30 percent of the time. You want to generate some kind of action from your contact to introduce you to the new person.

5. Teach Your Contacts How to Give You a Proper Referral

When you request a referral, ask your contact to call the potential referral, tell them about you and your services, and request permission for you to call. Tell your contact that if the referral source does not want to accept your call, it is OK. Closing percentages for a good referral are about 50 percent.

6. Take the Next Step and Ask for a Personal Introduction

If a contact is willing to make a referral to you, offer to set up a breakfast or lunch with your contact *and* the referral. Personal introductions turn into business 80-90 percent of the time.

7. Follow up with Your Referral Source

When you receive a referral, it is your responsibility to report on what happened. You want to give the referring party positive reinforcement, so that you will get more referrals in the future. Keep your referral sources happy! If someone gives you a referral, recognize the person with a "thank you," a note, or some other token of your appreciation.

8. Track Your Strategic Partnerships and Referral Groups

If you are not receiving referrals from your time investments in these relationships, you may want to replace them with new ones.

9. Do Not Pressure Someone Who Is Not Comfortable Giving Referrals

This point is worth emphasizing. You never want to jeopardize current relationships, so if someone is not comfortable giving referrals, do not push.

HOW TO ASK FOR REFERRALS

The best approach is simply to ask, honestly and directly, in a way that is authentic to you.

CASE IN POINT

Juan, a client from a prominent tax accounting firm, came to us because his firm insisted that he participate in our training program. He was not happy about this because he was very resistant to the idea of taking on responsibility for business development. The first thing we asked him to do was to begin asking his current clients for referrals. This idea was horrifying to him, but after we coached him through the process, he gave in and agreed to ask his two largest clients for a referral.

In keeping with the principle of saying what you are feeling, we coached Juan to tell his clients that he was embarrassed to ask, and he was sure they would not have any referrals for him, but that he was being forced to ask. The clients both responded that they thought the firm had all the business they needed and could not handle any more work, and they were more than happy to make introductions for him. As a result, he brought in more new business than any other accountant in the firm that year.

We asked Juan to step way out of his comfort zone, and he did. He was rewarded handsomely. No one was more surprised than he was!

The Gentle Approach

When asking for a referral, tonality is the key. You never want to come across as pushy or aggressive. If someone cannot come up with a referral for you, ask them gently for permission to ask a few questions. Then ask such questions as: Who are your five largest clients? Who are your five largest vendors (people who sell to them)? Who are the five top business associates with whom you interact?

Your ABCs

Another methodology is the ABC method, which is to take all of your contacts — business, social, etc. — and break them down into three categories, a tactic we covered in chapter ten. As you will recall, your "A" list consists of those people who will likely call you back within 48 hours. Your "B" list are those who will call you back within one week. The "C" list is everybody else.

Our most successful clients set a goal for how many people each week they will call from each list. When you have those conversations, you want to have them primarily with those people on your "A" and "B" lists. In general, our clients find that for every referral conversation they have with one of their contacts, it leads them to *two* conversations with people outside of their current network.

Asking for referrals can be difficult at first, but if it is done in the right way, the rewards you receive will condition you to become much more comfortable with the process. Not only will you grow your book of business, but you will free up a lot of your time because you will not need to do as much outside prospecting, and you can better service all of your clients – a win-win situation for all.

In the next chapter, we will discuss the value of social media platforms in business development.

Recap: Nine Tips for Increasing Referrals

1. Ask for referrals, even though doing so lies outside of your comfort zone.
2. Understand your target market.
3. Create a target list.
4. Do not accept a lead instead of a referral.
5. Teach your contacts how to give you a proper referral.
6. Take the next step and ask for a personal introduction.
7. Follow up with your referral source.
8. Track your strategic partnerships and referral groups.
9. Do not pressure someone who is not comfortable giving referrals.

CHAPTER THIRTEEN

Leveraging Social Media

"I do not have time to play around online."

Today, there is a new and powerful tool allowing professionals to become far more effective at targeting potential clients and developing a brand around their business: social media.

Social media, by definition, is an interaction among people in which they create, share, and exchange information and ideas in virtual communities and networks. There are several big picture reasons why the most successful professionals use social media to connect with people.

First, many professionals use social media as a direct and (potentially) inexpensive way to communicate their message. Social media is so powerful that in just a few keystrokes, your message can be delivered to thousands or even millions of people.

Second, professionals can use social media to collaborate with colleagues or to share ideas with their co-workers, project teams, prospects, and clients.

Yet another way that successful professionals utilize social media is to share videos, photos, and ideas. Some may use a site like YouTube to bring their ideas to life, demonstrate their expertise, or even show off their individuality to prospects and clients. Currently, there are a number of law firms who deliver seminars through YouTube videos.

As if that were not enough, professionals are now using their Web sites and mobile applications to differentiate themselves from the competition. They distinguish themselves by connecting with people in unique ways with a unique message. They use social media to create a more "personalized" experience for the people with whom they are trying to connect.

Some or all of these options may make sense in your world. It is time to focus in on some of the social media tools that help you open up the lines of communication between you and your current clients, former clients, network of contacts, and potential clients. Even if you are already using one of these platforms, please read all of the brief overviews that follow. You may spot a new idea you have not yet implemented!

LINKEDIN

LinkedIn is the world's largest professional online network with over 300,000,000 members in over 200 countries and territories. There are several important business development goals that can be accomplished by utilizing LinkedIn.

First, LinkedIn can help you connect easily with the people in your network who you would like to stay in front of, but do not have the time to personally contact. On this platform, you can post articles, track the current events of people in your network, and connect with others in a quick and inexpensive manner. If you are able to invest fifteen to twenty minutes per day, you can browse LinkedIn to stay on top of what is happening with all or nearly all of the people in your network.

Next, you can use LinkedIn to proactively ask for referrals from people who are in your network. Once you have determined that you are going to ask a specific person for a referral, navigate the connections section in their profile. When you view somebody's connections, you can see who is in his network and get an overview of what the people in his network do for a living. Once you view someone's connections, you can be more precise in asking for referrals.

We find that when you research someone's connection before a meeting in which you will be asking for referrals, you will receive an average of three referrals per meeting.

You can use the search function within LinkedIn to target specific companies and specific individuals to identify people in your own network who can connect you with the individual you would like to meet.

Many professionals use LinkedIn to research potential clients. If you view someone's LinkedIn profile, you can glean information such as where the person went to school, worked, or contributed as a member of a professional association. You can also find out about other interests both inside and outside of the business world. If you use this information in the right way, you can easily warm up a cold call or a first meeting.

LinkedIn can also be used to search for professionals with whom you have attributes in common, such as where you went to school and what groups you have joined. This feature can help you find a common thread within groups of individuals or organizations you are looking to target.

CASE IN POINT

The senior executives of a specialty engineering firm had conducted research and found that a large project was coming up from an organization with whom they had wanted to work for some time. The project would be ideal for them and they knew the names of the people who were on the committee to award the work — but they did not have relationships with any of the decision makers.

At our suggestion, each of the partners at the engineering firm used LinkedIn to find out whether people in their network could help make introductions for them. Each of the principals from the engineering firm had at least two contacts who had relationships with the decision makers awarding the project. The engineering firm made calls to their contacts, and in turn, their contacts reached out to the decision makers from the firm awarding the work. The engineering firm's contacts all spoke about the great work that the engineering firm had done, and they recommended that the decision makers meet with the engineering firm before awarding the work.

This organization received calls from *five* different sources talking about the great work that this engineering firm provided. The target firm met with our client, and ultimately the engineering firm was awarded the work. They were told that the biggest contributing factor to winning the work was the phone calls that people made on their behalf.

Consider, too, that LinkedIn can be used to establish your credibility. LinkedIn provides you with a venue to post your articles, your ideas, and your content. You can join specific industry groups though LinkedIn to ensure that your ideas are getting in front of your target market. When used intelligently and on a regular basis, LinkedIn can help you establish yourself as an expert to the people you are trying to meet. And if you have a good LinkedIn strategy, you can convert a digital conversation into a real conversation.

We would suggest that you create specific goals for using LinkedIn, and track your behavior to determine which tactics are working and which tactics are not. Like so many of today's interactive media platforms, LinkedIn can become a "time sinkhole" if you do not carefully monitor and analyze the results you generate. (That goes for all the platforms you will be reading about here.)

TWITTER

Twitter is a microblogging platform that has become increasingly popular in recent years. Twitter allows you to post your thoughts and ideas in 140 characters or less through your computer or smartphone. Today, professionals utilize Twitter to connect with people, express themselves, and stay current on trending topics.

If you do decide to use Twitter to demonstrate your expertise, it is important to have a strategy before you begin. Ask yourself questions such as, "What do I want to accomplish?" and "How will I know if I am being successful with this platform?"

In addition, it is important to make Twitter a consistent behavior. In our experience, you need to commit to posting items at least several times per week if you hope to gain traction on Twitter.

CASE IN POINT

Steve is a class action attorney. In order to be successful, Steve needs to attract hundreds or thousands of clients for an individual case. On many occasions, Steve has used Twitter as a platform to attract potential clients. In less than 140 characters, he can relay to the world (appropriate, non-sensitive) information about the litigation that he's pursuing. Guess what happens? Rather than him trying to seek out the potential clients, potential clients find *him* after he posts on Twitter and LinkedIn!

Blogs

The word "blog" comes from the phrase "Web log." Blogs are articles posted via such platforms as Blogger. This is another tool professionals can use to establish credibility and develop a good reputation online.

A blog is basically a Web site devoted to your online articles. Some professionals will host a blog on their Web site, and other professionals will post articles and comment on articles on a variety of Web sites. Writing and commenting on blogs will allow others to see your expertise and help you build your brand. Many savvy professionals will post their blogs and comments in places online where their potential clients can see them. A great blog post can cause a potential client to call you! This tool can be especially effective if you operate in a very specialized area.

CASE IN POINT

Tom is an attorney who focuses on education and working within schools and with school boards. Tom started blogging two to three times per week on topics focused on education.

Tom did not hear anything at first, but after several months he began receiving a steady stream of calls and email inquiries based on his blog entries. Here again, consistency counts. Tom posted at least two articles a week, and he kept it up. He went from being an associate who was developing no business to being a rainmaker in a little less than one year, primarily through the power of social media. Of course, not everyone is capable of composing compelling blog copy or establishing extensive social media contacts. You should expect the results of efforts like these to correlate to your writing and social media networking skills.

The Real You

No matter what social media platform you choose for your business and personal brand there are three crucial things to remember: Be real. Be focused. Be consistent.

For a business or business professional brand, it is vital to be both authentic and clear about what you want to communicate. With every tweet, post, like, or comment, you should incorporate your true personality, passion, and style — as a professional. People may interact with your messages in a virtual world, but they will connect with you as an individual for being real!

Focus. Communicate about issues that are relevant to your target audience. Do not mix your personal information with your business observations.

Remember that winning clients and building loyalty does not happen overnight. No matter what tools you identify as best for your professional brand and organization, consistency is the key to success. Building strong relationships online requires an ongoing, consistent effort that will provide brand recognition and confidence.

LESS IS MORE

Social media tools can be overwhelming and exhausting. Find the best tools and platforms for you, then stick to those. Do not try to create a presence on every possible platform in order be visible everywhere. That is not feasible – or necessary.

An effective social media plan must be focused and targeted to where your audience and ideal community is going to find their information. That means you must identify which platform holds the top conversations in your industry. That is where you want to stake your claim. You want to be where the most targeted contacts are, so you can communicate and share your information with them — not with everyone on earth!

> Use social media to get your name and message in front of current clients and potential prospects. Use it to start conversations with new prospects and stay relevant with current clients. Track the results from your time and effort on social media, so that you can determine your own return on investment. Do not keep investing time and money on platforms that are not paying off.

In the next chapter, we will cover advanced prospecting techniques.

Recap: Social Media

- Be real.
- Be focused.
- Be consistent.
- Track your results.
- Do not keep investing time and money on platforms that are not paying off.

CHAPTER FOURTEEN

Advanced Prospecting Techniques: Workshops, Seminars, and Peer Groups

"This is the way we have always done it."

Over the years, one of the most consistent complaints we hear from professional service firms and their marketing directors is that they invest thousands of dollars and countless hours on seminars and conferences that do not lead to new business. We hear horror stories from professionals who attend these events and then tell us that they do not make contacts, arrange meetings, or produce any new opportunities. We also hear from professionals who deliver seminars and do not generate the number of prospects they had anticipated. How can you avoid having experiences like those?

CASE IN POINT

We worked with a law firm many years ago, and coached one of their attorneys. We'll call her Linda.

Linda was very proud of the fact that she was one of the best-known speakers in the Eastern United States on a particular topic, and that at least once per month she was asked to give a talk regarding that topic. When we asked Linda how much business she developed from all of these speaking opportunities, her response was that no business had come from the events, but that she had shared important and timely content. She was sure that if a need for her services came about, she would be receiving a phone call from the participants in the workshop.

We asked Linda whether there was any internal pressure from her firm because the workshops were costing money and utilizing internal resources without generating new clients. Linda admitted that she was getting pressure from her firm to develop business, so we asked if she was open to making changes to her workshop. After a few conversations, Linda agreed to change the format.

Since Linda delivered the same workshop for every group, we suggested that she send out a survey to the workshop participants one week *before* the workshop to determine which sub-topics interested the participants the most. In addition, we suggested that at the beginning of the workshop, she ask the audience what they wanted to hear during the course of the workshop, and what their biggest questions and challenges around that topic were. Next, rather than overloading the audience with content, we suggested that Linda speak about the highlights of the subjects the audience requested, but not delve too deeply into those topics. In addition, rather than strictly answering questions, Linda began asking the participants *why* they brought up specific topics, and how those topics were impacting their businesses.

Overnight, Linda went from speaking 95 percent of the time at these seminars, to having her audience speak about their issues for over half of the seminar. In addition, challenges that one participant was experiencing would provide an opportunity for other participants to share how they were dealing with similar challenges.

At the end of the workshop, Linda handed out a survey to determine which of the participants wanted her to follow up with them in more detail. As soon as Linda changed the format, she began to receive three to four requests for follow-up meetings after each seminar. In the first six months after she changed her seminar format, she developed eight new clients from her seminars. Those eight new clients, eight more than she had developed in the previous eighteen months, resulted in over $500,000 in new business growth.

You can maximize your results from seminars and conferences if you learn how to plan and work them correctly in order to uncover new business opportunities. If you commit to developing a plan, investing time and effort to execute your plan, and tracking the results of your efforts, you will be rewarded with new business and relevant contacts.

ATTENDING CONFERENCES AND TRADE SHOWS

The first thing you must do if you are going to attend conferences and trade shows is define your target market.

Many professional service firms and marketing directors report being disappointed with the results of a trade show or seminar. When we ask about the goals they were hoping to achieve at these events, we hear statements like, "We have always participated in that conference," or "All of our competitors are there." Sometimes, no target audience has even been identified!

If you or your firm are going to invest the time and money to attend a conference or trade show, you must have an understanding as to whom you want to target, whether those people will be in attendance, and what goals or outcomes you want to accomplish from the conferences or seminars you attend.

Preparing Your Message

Before you leave for the conference or trade show, it is important to make sure you have a clearly defined message to deliver when you meet new people. A conference or trade show is the ideal opportunity for you to utilize your 30-second commercial. It is important to do your research *before* leaving for the conference or trade show so that you can tailor your message to the people you meet.

For most professionals, it is important to have several different 30-second commercials prepared for the conference or trade show.

The Big Picture

First, you should have a 30-second commercial that discusses the types of problems your firm helps its best clients overcome. This commercial should be a more general commercial that provides prospects with an overview of the ways that you can help your clients succeed. Until you learn more details about the person you are meeting, it is good to provide a general overview and discuss the big picture problems that you help your clients overcome.

If you have a narrow specialty, the general population may not have a need for your service. For example, if you are a forensic accountant and you attend a general trade show, there may not be many companies who are in need of a forensic accountant at that time. If you were to just talk about your specialty, you might not have much luck finding new prospects. On the other hand, if you happen to work in a multi-disciplinary firm, you may be able to discuss the general business problems that the firm helps clients overcome, which might include tax and audit work.

All About You

The second type of commercial that you should prepare before leaving for a conference or trade show is a commercial that highlights your specialty. Once you identify that the person with whom you are speaking has a need for your specific services, you can be more specific when talking about the problems you solve for your clients.

Make sure that when you give a more focused commercial about your specific area, you focus on the potential problems that your prospect is running into rather than listing out your features and benefits. You may want to include one or two brief stories about how you have helped specific people.

Strategic Partners

The last type of commercial you should prepare before leaving for a conference or a trade show is a commercial that is targeted toward potential strategic partners.

You should think about what types of companies or what types of professionals might be a good potential partner, and focus on the problems that you could solve for their clients. In addition, be prepared to talk about ways in which you could partner with different professionals. For many professionals, leaving a conference with two or three good potential strategic partners could be as effective as walking away with the same number of new business opportunities.

CASE IN POINT

For each of the five years before beginning work with us, one of our clients had been sending three to five consultants to a trade conference in Las Vegas. They had never been able to account for a single new client, or any return on their investment of time and money, as a result of attending that conference.

When the conference appeared on the calendar, we took the time to strategize a different approach. This time, we suggested that each consultant target twenty people on the conference attendance list that they believed would be potential contacts for future projects.

We asked that they try to reach out and schedule meetings before they even left for the conference, so that they would have appointments set up in advance and would not need to depend on "bumping into" the right contacts. We suggested the best time to plan these meetings would be either for breakfast (you can schedule multiple breakfast meetings each morning), lunch, or cocktails after the conference. We also advised that the best way to set up these meetings was via email and phone calls, and that they needed to start three to four weeks before the conference was scheduled.

Before making the calls, we had the consultants research the contacts on LinkedIn to determine whether they could get introduced to their targeted contacts by a shared contact, rather than making cold calls and sending cold emails in advance. We also strongly urged them not be afraid to email people they had never met before and ask whether they would be attending a specific upcoming conference event, in order to determine whether the person would be open to scheduling a time to speak.

As a result of implementing these suggestions, the four consultants who attended the conference that year made fifteen new contacts, and shortly after the conference, they developed four new clients.

Once they were able to make a plan and try something new, they realized different (and much better) results.

Provide a Talk or Seminar at a Conference or Trade Show

Our next suggestion for developing business is to deliver a talk or become part of a panel for one of the sessions at a seminar or trade show.

At conferences and seminars, no one gets as much attention as the speaker. Most conferences and seminars are actively looking for speakers. Develop a seminar based on the problems you solve, and research conferences where your talk would be appropriate. Once you are able to fill this role, participants of the conference will be seeking you out!

Reach out in Advance

Before you deliver your seminar, there are several tactics you can employ to ensure that you are able to develop business as a result of your talk. First, obtain a list of attendees for the conference. A few weeks before the conference, make phone calls to the people you would like to meet at the conference. During the phone call, share the topic that you will be speaking about, and ask your target prospects to provide their thoughts on the topic. Ask if they would like to see any additional content added to the talk. Finally, make sure that you invite the prospects to attend your talk.

Typically, when you reach out to people to get their opinion and feedback, those people will be flattered. They will now be personally connected to you and your talk, and the chances that they will attend your talk will dramatically increase. In addition, you will find that these people will seek you out after your talk to give you feedback. This is a great way to start a relationship with a potential client.

Make It Memorable

The key to any talk or seminar is to make it as interactive as possible. It is not the content, but the entertainment value that people are most likely to remember. Through how many boring seminars and conferences have you suffered? How much information did you retain from those seminars? If you keep the audience entertained and make them feel comfortable with your expertise on a topic, you will develop new opportunities.

Follow Up

After the conference or seminar, *follow up, follow up, and follow up some more.*

> The biggest mistake you can make after a conference or seminar is to return immediately to your regular daily routine, rather than following up with your new contacts immediately after the event.

If you work a conference correctly, you will be making many new contacts and it will be very difficult to remember each person you meet and every conversation. After you meet each new contact or complete a meeting, write a note in your smartphone or on the back of their business card. Note something that will remind you what the person looks like and the conversation you had.

When you meet someone at the event, ask permission to follow up. If you get permission to follow up, ask how and when you should reconnect. Do you need to make a call, send information, or check in by email? What will you talk about when you call? You need to plan to complete your follow-up activities no later than one week following the event you attended or the talk you provided. If you do not follow up within one week of the event, the potency of the contact will be lost.

Return on Investment

Finally, it is important to measure your ROI (return on investment).

Make sure that after you attend an event, you develop a system to track the return on investment for that event. How much did the event cost your firm? How much time did you spend away from the office while attending the event? If you were a speaker, how much time did it take you to prepare? What type of follow up did you do? How effective was it? Identify the amount of new business or new contacts that originated from the event.

Did you pick up new opportunities from old clients? Did you develop new relationships? How much were they worth? The results may surprise you.

PEER GROUPS

We define a peer group as a group of professionals who meet on a regular basis (usually weekly or monthly) for the sole purpose of trying to provide referrals and introductions for each other.

In the ideal peer group, there are other professionals within the group who are a natural complement to what you do. Typically, there are no members of the group who provide the same services that you provide.

There are many different types of peer groups. There are formal peer groups run by national organizations and less formal groups created by individuals. When looking for a peer group, it is important to find the right mix of people who are targeting the same types of professionals you are looking to meet, and who are in the position to make referrals and introductions for you.

GET CREATIVE!

There are many different non-traditional prospecting activities you can use as you grow your business — far more than we have listed here. Use your own creativity to identify opportunities that make sense for your organization. Here again, you will find that the key to success with prospecting is to have a plan, work your plan, track results, and find someone who will hold you accountable. Once you begin to work your plan, you will find that positive results will follow.

In the next chapter, we will talk about return on investment and how to measure it.

Recap: Tips for Business-Building Seminars

- **Reach out in advance** – Before you deliver your seminar, get a list of attendees for the conference and make phone calls to the people who you would like to meet.
- **Make it memorable** – If you keep the audience entertained, and you make them feel comfortable with your expertise on a topic, you will develop new opportunities.
- **Follow up** – The biggest mistake that can be made after a conference or seminar is to return to your regular daily activities and not follow up with your new contacts immediately after the event.
- **Return on Investment** – Develop a system to track the return on investment for each event.

CHAPTER FIFTEEN

Measuring Return on Investment for All of Your Prospecting Activities

"This all sounds great. But how do I know whether it is working?"

Now that you have set your SMART goals (chapter four), defined your ideal target clients (chapter six), determined the amount of time and money you can invest on your prospecting plan (chapter seven), and implemented a number of different prospecting ideas (chapters eight through fourteen), it is time to track the results of your prospecting plan.

When you track your return on investment (ROI), there are three parts of the business development cycle that you should be evaluating.

WHAT'S COOKING?

First, it is important to set behavior goals for the prospecting activities that you will put into your plan, so you can take the steps needed to achieve those goals. At Sandler Training, we call these business development activities your Behavior Cookbook (see the text box below).

We suggest that you begin your behavior cookbook by looking at the amount of revenue you want to generate over the course of the next twelve months. You should then work backwards from that revenue goal to determine the number of clients or number of new projects you need to close in order to reach those revenue goals.

Once you determine the number of clients you need to close, you must look at what your closing percentage is once you reach a final meeting or submit a proposal on a new project. This number will help you to determine the number of closing meetings you will need in order to generate enough new projects or clients to execute your plan successfully.

For example, if you determine that you need to find five new clients over the course of the year, and your closing percentage, once you have a final meeting or submit a proposal, is 50 percent, then you will need ten closing meetings or proposals to generate five new clients.

Next, we suggest you look at the behavior needed to generate ten closing meetings. If one out of three first meetings or initial consults results in a qualified prospect, you may need to have thirty first meetings over the course of the year to generate ten closing meetings, that will in turn generate five new clients.

Once you complete the exercise below, you will have created your own behavior cookbook. Follow it!

Behavior Cookbook

Revenue Generated Over Next 12 Months	_____
Average Value of a New Client	_____
Number of Clients Needed	_____
Number of Closing Meetings Needed	_____
Number of First Meetings Needed	_____

When prospecting, you cannot control the outcome of a meeting — because there is no foolproof way to determine whether your prospect is qualified before the first meeting. You can, however, control your behavior.

WHAT TO DO AND WHEN TO DO IT

It is not only important to know *what* prospecting activities you need to perform in order to reach your goals; you also need to establish *when* those activities need to happen.

We recommend breaking your prospecting activities into daily, weekly, monthly, and quarterly activities. It is also important that your activities be consistent with those required by your cookbook in order to stay on track and achieve your goals.

Track your behavior over time. You may find that as you implement the techniques from this book, your closing percentages improve and you will not need to generate as much activity to achieve your goals. However, if the economy dips, or if a market dries up, those same goals may require more activity.

Another advantage of tracking ROI is to provide you with a roadmap of the behaviors you should implement as you move forward in order to consistently achieve your goals.

If you are having a really good month or a really good quarter — and you are tracking your behavior — you will be able to replicate those activities over and over again. If you find that you are not achieving your goals, you can determine why those goals are not being achieved, and you can change your behavior to get better results.

Professionals who do not track their behavior will have a difficult time predicting the results of their behavior and managing their business and project pipeline.

But tracking your behaviors is only half the battle. Now that you have completed your behavior cookbook, scheduled your behaviors, and begun to track them, you will also need to track and measure the *effectiveness* of your prospecting plan.

LEADING INDICATORS

The first thing you want to look at when tracking the effectiveness of your plan is your leading indicators. Leading indicators are the results that you are achieving at the beginning of the business development pipeline, and those leading indicators will be able to help you determine the amount of business that will close in the future.

CASE IN POINT

John was the Managing Director of a consulting firm, and he was frustrated because he did not know what new projects would create business from month to month, and was therefore having a difficult time managing his resources and his business pipeline.

We sat down with John and looked at the business he had developed and the factors that put opportunities into his business pipeline. As we worked with John, we discovered that the number of referrals he received, the number of unique prospects that he reached out to each month, the number of first meetings that he scheduled with new prospective clients each month, and the number of proposals that went out each month would collectively give him a good idea of the results that he could expect over the next 60 to 90 days. John determined that if he met with three new opportunities per week and generated one new proposal per week for a qualified prospect, there was a very good chance that he would exceed his revenue goals.

LAGGING INDICATORS

The next factors to look at when measuring ROI are your lagging indicators.

The lagging indicators are the results achieved after you have completed your activity. Lagging indicators may include the amount of new business that has been closed, the revenue generated from the business that has been closed, the amount of time it takes from first contact to closing the business, and the profit margin from new business.

CASE IN POINT

Michael was the managing partner of a large architectural firm. His firm worked in several different market segments. Michael was frustrated because his people were busy and the firm was generating what seemed like a fair amount of revenue, but there was not much profit to distribute to the partners at the end of the year.

When we sat down with Michael and reviewed his numbers, we found that 40 percent of the firm's revenue came from working on projects for the state and federal governments. The problem was that the bidding process had created an environment in which the firm barely broke even on those projects. In addition, Michael saw that those projects for the government also took a longer period of time to get paid than the other types of projects that the firm completed.

Once Michael reviewed the numbers, the firm changed their strategy and stayed out of the government marketplace. The following year, revenues for the firm increased slightly, but the firm's profit margin increased significantly.

Archaeological Prospecting

There is one final exercise that we strongly suggest that you complete. This exercise will provide you with a good roadmap of the prospecting activities you should engage in to achieve your goals. We suggest you go back through the business you have generated over the past three to five years and track which prospecting activities led to a relationship with each client. Set out on an archaeological expedition!

How much business have you generated through referrals, up-selling, and cross-selling? How much business have you generated by responding to RFPs and RFQs? Has your firm presented any workshops or seminars, and did those activities lead to new business? Did you invest time and money in sponsorships or professional associations that did not lead to business? Are there certain activities that you should stop doing because they are not generating new business?

We suggest that you take a look at your cookbook, your prospect pipeline, and the business that you have closed on a weekly or monthly (at a minimum) basis. Look at what is working, what is not working, and what needs to be changed.

Once you have a plan and commit that plan to writing, it will be much easier for you to predict your results and make the proper changes to ensure your success in developing new business.

In the next chapter, we will discuss techniques you can implement once you are in front of a new opportunity that will allow you to demonstrate your expertise without providing free consulting.

Recap: Measuring Return on Investment

- Create and follow a Behavior Cookbook.
- Track both leading indicators and lagging indicators.
- Conduct occasional archaeological prospecting expeditions.
- Remember: When prospecting, you cannot control the outcome of a meeting — because there is no foolproof way to determine whether your prospect is qualified before the first meeting. You can, however, control your behavior.

CHAPTER SIXTEEN

Unpaid Consulting

"How am I supposed to demonstrate my expertise?"

When a prospect or a suspect (i.e., an unqualified prospect) asks you for free information, do you provide it? If your answer is "Yes," you are an *unpaid consultant*.

If a potential client asks you to help him or her figure out the solution to a problem, and you joyfully and confidently respond with your solution to that problem before getting a commitment – you are an *unpaid consultant*.

When you are asked for your fees and you do not have a thorough understanding of not only what they want, but *why* they want that specific product or service — but you offer a quote anyway — you are an *unpaid consultant*.

If you are giving away proprietary firm information for free, without any commitment – *you are definitely an unpaid consultant*.

Unless you are in the restaurant business, you should not be giving away your product or service prior to getting a commitment from your client to purchase. Providing free consulting before qualifying your prospect is the wrong place and the wrong time to present your proprietary information. Providing a premature presentation is how you create "Head Trash" (thoughts and emotions that create fear and prevent us from operating as intelligently as we normally would) and water down the marketplace. In addition, you could be doing a disservice to your prospect by providing them with free consulting before you fully understand their needs, their challenges, and their motivation for making a decision.

CASE IN POINT

Ken is an engineer who worked for a large construction management firm. Occasionally, Ken would get a request from a "strategic partner" or prospective client for a quote. Some of his partners would call him with a very tight deadline, and they would present him with a difficult issue. Some of those partners would ask him for possible solutions to attack the problem, and they would request a quote for his firm to work on the project. Typically, to provide an answer to the questions he was hearing, Ken would need to coordinate with several internal resources, and it would take several hours for him and his team to turn around a quote or proposal.

When we asked Ken how often these opportunities developed into new business, he said he had no idea. After we asked him to go back and track the results, he found that only 15 percent of these opportunities developed into new business, and that when his firm did win the business, it was at a lower than normal profit margin.

When we asked him to take a deeper look at the numbers, he found that four different organizations had made emergency requests for proposals multiple times (a total of 22 quick turnaround proposals) and had never used his services. At my request, the next time Ken was asked for a quote from one of those organizations, he asked his prospect why they kept calling him for his expertise since he never was awarded the business.

At first the prospect did not want to answer, but after Ken pressed the point, he discovered that the person who was requesting the free consulting was regularly using one of Ken's competitors! This prospect found that Ken's competitors were always quoting rates that were too high, so they would get Ken's proposals to drive down the fees of their current provider. In addition, Ken's prospect shared that they did not trust the incumbent provider to give them the best solutions to the most complex issues, so they would share Ken's suggestions with the incumbent provider, and then have that competitor implement Ken's ideas at a cheaper fee.

Ken, feeling more than a little angry and upset at this point, asked what he would need to do to win the business. He discovered that the owner of the firm was golfing buddies with the competitor, and although the technical people were not happy with the work, nothing was going to interfere with the owner's relationship with that provider.

WHY BUY THE COW?

When you provide your expertise, ideas, fees, unique characteristics, etc. before you get a commitment from your prospect, you are seriously jeopardizing your chance to successfully land that client. Prospects will use the free consulting you give them against you by either shopping the information around to your competitors, or by trying to take your information and implement your ideas themselves.

If you give prospects your pricing structure up front, they will of course try to make money the major issue. (Money never is the major issue, by the way–but we will cover that in the Pain and Budget chapters.) When you give people your unique ideas and/or product characteristics, what is to stop them from sharing all of that with their current provider to determine whether they can deliver similar services?

In all of those cases, your "prospects" will have no compelling reason to work with you.

The truly professional strategic advisor will not provide consulting of any substance without first closing the deal, or at least getting a commitment from the prospect. The first step in getting that commitment is to establish effective bonding and rapport with the prospect while also building trust (see chapter 17 on Bonding and Building Rapport).

Your prospect needs to feel confident that you truly understand not only their intellectual needs, but also their emotional involvement in those intellectual needs. Once you are there, the prospect will have the trust and confidence that you are the one to solve their pressing issues. You accomplish this by asking the right questions, listening intently, and then questioning some more.

Remember: Truly professional business development requires that you listen 70 percent of the time and talk only 30 percent of the time!

SEEING THE WHOLE PICTURE

If you are providing free consulting for your prospects too early in the process, you are not only jeopardizing your chances of winning the business, but you may be doing a disservice to your prospects.

How often has this scenario happened to you? A prospective client initiates a conversation with you and presents you with a specific challenge. You enter into an agreement, based on the issues that your prospective client presented to you, and as you begin to work with the client, you find that the issue they initially brought to you is not the real issue, but a symptom of a larger issue.

You may find that sometimes a prospect does this because they have never dealt with the issue before and they did not realize that what they were initially seeing was part of a larger issue. Other times, you may find that some prospects were less than honest with you and did not provide you with the true issues up front, and may have minimized their issues so that you would quote a lower fee.

> **CASE IN POINT**
>
> One of our clients, David, is an architect who builds homes and provides additions for homeowners. David was talking to a prospective client who was interested in building an addition to her home. The owner of the home had never experienced a project like this, and she assumed that it would be a simple process. As David talked with her further, he discovered that she did not realize she would need to secure permits, that evaluations would need to be performed regarding the structure of the home to ensure safety, and that the plans she had acquired 20 years ago were no longer up to code — meaning that the project would need to be started from scratch.
>
> In addition, if David had not asked good questions up front, he would not have realized that the homeowner's budget was only 25 percent of what was needed to complete the project. David was able to discover these details in a first meeting, however, and as a result he immediately disqualified the prospect.
>
> When we asked David how much time he saved himself by not providing free consulting, he shared that he had saved over 20 hours of his time, and that extra time allowed him to get in front of two other qualified prospects.

Tell Me Where It Hurts

The analogy that we like to use with our clients regarding their first meeting with a prospect is to compare it to a visit to the doctor's office with symptoms of an illness. Let us pretend that you went to your doctor's office with a stomach ache. Would your doctor immediately suggest cutting you open in the office and starting an involved medical procedure, or would the doctor ask questions and perform some tests before presenting you with a diagnosis and a course of treatment? What would happen to the doctor who just started prescribing medication or providing medical procedures without first going through a discovery process to identify the real issues?

Unfortunately, we often find that people who are experts in their field will jump in and try to provide a solution to one of their prospective clients before asking questions to fully diagnose what the real issues are, how the issues will impact the client, and how the prospective client would prefer to handle the issue. The reason we try to jump in and provide solutions up front is that we have been conditioned to do so our entire lives. When growing up, kids were rewarded in school and at home by knowing the right answers to questions. Typically, people show off their knowledge by jumping in with solutions.

Our experience shows us that using your expertise to ask your prospects good questions will provide you with more credibility than trying to immediately answer every question they present to you. For many of our clients, there are many different solutions that they could provide to their clients, and they find that different clients have different needs or preferences.

CASE IN POINT

One of our clients, a litigation attorney named Joe, found that some of his clients wanted litigation to go away quickly and quietly, and they were willing to make early settlements in order to minimize publicity. Joe had other clients who wanted to win their litigation cases at all costs, and they would refuse to settle because they thought it would set a bad precedent.

If Joe did not question his prospective clients about their thoughts regarding litigation, he might present a "win at all costs" strategy to a client who just wants litigation to go away, or he might present a "let's settle and get this over with" strategy to someone who wants to win at all costs. Joe is successful in implementing both strategies, but he needs to ask his clients strategic questions to discover which strategy each client is most comfortable pursuing.

CASE IN POINT

Many of our clients need to develop business by taking business away from their competitors.

Mary is a partner in a small consulting firm who works with Fortune 100 companies. Mary was called in to meet with a client she knew was working with one of her largest competitors. When Mary met with the client, she asked what the client was hoping to bring away from their meeting.

The client started off by saying that they were looking at different consulting firms because the company might be open to making a change. The client asked Mary how they would work with a Fortune 100 company. If Mary had just jumped in and answered the question, she might have discussed strategies or a roll out that the client was not comfortable implementing. Instead of answering the question, Mary asked the person what they liked and did not like about the consulting firms they had worked with in the past.

The Fortune 100 client spent the next 30 minutes describing what they liked and did not like about their previous relationships. Asking this question gave Mary valuable insight that she never would have discovered simply through researching the company. When the prospective client finished speaking, Mary was able to position her answer in a way that made her prospective client very comfortable. Thirty days after the initial meeting, Mary had a contract to work with that company.

It is important to have a business development process that will allow you, rather than your prospect, to stay in control of the situation.

You will find that you have greater success if you allow your clients to share with you what they are looking for, rather than you blindly providing solutions. Your process should require that your prospect *qualifies* to get a proposal/presentation/advice from you. In order to qualify, they must have "pain" (problems they have that you can solve) and the appropriate budget needed to solve those problems, and you must know everything there is to know about their decision-making process.

When you implement a strong business development process, you will no longer be a free consultant and your business will grow as it never has before.

In the next part of the book, you will begin to learn about the Sandler Submarine. This powerful business development model begins with Bonding and Rapport.

Recap: Free Consulting

If you are providing free consulting for your prospects too early in the process, you are not only jeopardizing your chances of winning the business, but you may also be doing a disservice to your prospects.

PART THREE:
*A Systematic Approach
to Developing Business*

CHAPTER SEVENTEEN

Bonding and Rapport

"Where do I start?"

Meeting and identifying a potential client is only half the battle. Once we have utilized our prospecting techniques to target a qualified prospect and convinced the qualified prospect to agree to a meeting, we need a process for moving the conversation forward and, eventually, closing and securing the deal.

Over the next seven chapters, we will introduce you to the Sandler methodology of developing business, known as the Sandler Selling System, which is depicted by the Sandler Submarine. The submarine has seven compartments. We will be looking at the first of those compartments, Bonding and Rapport, in this chapter.

For many professionals, developing business is challenging. Many who have tried to develop business and failed will stop trying when they do not experience success. Often, that challenge and lack of success is the result of not having a reliable process in place. The "watertight" compartments of the Sandler Submarine give you that reliable process. If you master it, you will always know where you currently stand in the business development process, always know the next steps of the process, and never lose control of the opportunity.

When you do not have a process in place for business development, you

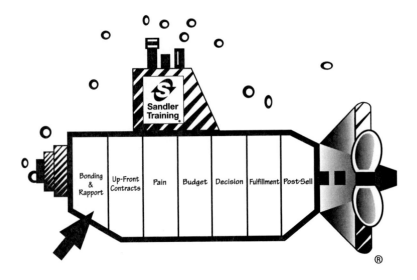

will find that some meetings go well while others are a total waste of time. For those of you who are trying to develop a team to help support your organization's business development efforts, putting a process in place will allow you to systematize your approach and will enable your entire team to utilize the same process. In addition, there will be consistency throughout the organization when it comes to qualifying opportunities.

The first step of the Sandler approach to business development is called Bonding and Rapport. We find that there are three rules of business that apply to Bonding and Rapport.

Rule #1 - People like to do business with people they like.
Rule #2 - People like to do business with people like themselves.
Rule #3 - Often it is not what you have or your expertise that leads to success — it is who you know.

The first part of your job, once you meet with a prospect, is to make your prospect comfortable. Put yourself in your prospect's shoes for a moment. If you sit down for a first meeting with someone and he begins by asking you difficult or personal questions in the initial five minutes, would that make you comfortable? If the consultant you were meeting with spent the first part of the meeting bragging about his successes and spouting the reasons why you need to work with him, would you want to work with that person?

For many attorneys, accountants, and professional consultants, you need to ask your potential clients difficult questions that might make them uncomfortable. If you do not build up trust and a relationship with your prospects, they either will not answer your questions, or they will not be truthful with you when they do answer your questions.

Our clients are successful in their meetings when they focus their attention on making the prospect feel comfortable. When you are in your role as a business developer, it is your responsibility to keep the prospect feeling comfortable with you. When developing rapport with someone, you want to focus on him.

Some of the ways that you might want to start the conversation could include asking your prospects about where they grew up, talking about people you both know, asking about where they went to school, or asking about their professional background. In general, we find a direct correlation between the amount of time that the prospect speaks and their comfort level with you. In an ideal world, the prospect should speak for approximately 70 percent of the meeting and you should speak for approximately 30 percent of the meeting. How much are you currently speaking in your meetings with potential clients?

When the prospect asks about you and your business, you may want to give an expanded version of your 30-second commercial. Talk about the problems that you solve for your clients rather than just providing a list of your services.

BEYOND THE WORDS

Many people concentrate so much on the words they want to use that they forget about the other important aspects of communication. Let us look at some of those right now.

Attire and Body Language

Think about the last time you were at a networking event. Was there somebody at the event who was dressed differently than everyone else? If so, did he stand out? We have seen people at an event dismiss someone strictly because of the way he was dressed. Many of the law firms we have worked with over the years have told us that they will not work with a salesperson or consultant who is not dressed in proper business attire. On the other hand, if you are a project manager or consultant working in the construction industry or with IT professionals and you show up on a work site, it might not be appropriate to wear a suit.

Your prospect will make judgments about your capabilities based on your image before they ever hear about your credentials. Body language includes everything from how you are dressed, to the amount of personal space that you give someone, to the way that you shake hands, to body posture and how people perceive you — and it has a huge effect on how we communicate with each other.

Have you ever been in a meeting with a person who seemed really laid back? Maybe that person was leaning back in his chair or had a very open posture. Do you think he would react well if you were leaning across the table or banging on the table to make a point?

How do you think that someone with a type A personality would react if you were too laid back in a meeting? Might he dismiss you because he does not believe that you are taking his problems seriously?

Have you ever been in a meeting with someone who was not making eye contact with you and had his arms crossed the entire time? Maybe he was not looking at you when he was speaking, or even worse he was texting on his phone.

It is important to pay attention to the physical cues that someone is presenting to you during a meeting. If you get the feeling that the meeting is not going well based on the physical cues that you are receiving, you can address the issue and inquire about where you went wrong.

Vocal Cues

The next way that we communicate with each other is through the tonality of our voice. Tonality speaks to how quickly or slowly you talk, the volume of your voice, and how much you modulate your voice.

Think back to the last time a telemarketer caught you at home at dinner time. How long did it take you to determine that it was a telemarketer on the phone? Have you recently been called at the office by a salesperson? If your experience is like that of most people, you were able to tell that it was a salesperson almost instantly (even if you did not use caller ID and the salesperson pronounced your name correctly).

Typically, we are able to identify a salesperson on the phone because he sounds scripted. Most of those people are either reading off a script or they have memorized one. Once we hear that voice on the phone, we tend to put our defenses up and screen the call.

Before we make calls, we need to remember how we perceive the typical salesperson, and then act completely different. You will have better luck keeping your prospect engaged in a conversation if you do not sound scripted than you would by memorizing a script.

For those of you who provide services on a national or international level, you know that people in different parts of the country and different parts of the world speak differently. If you are speaking slowly and deliberately to someone in New York, that person might dismiss you because he will believe that you are wasting his time by not speaking quickly enough. A person from the Northeast may need to slow his natural voice cadence if he is speaking with someone in the South or Midwest. Remember, when you are in a business development role, it is important to speak to your prospects and clients in the way that will make them the most comfortable.

When you speak, you should, of course, have a good working knowledge of your subject matter and be able to communicate your point of view to your client or prospect. But do not get lost in the words. Many people will spend hours making sure that their script is perfect, and then ruin that script by not matching the prospect's body language and tone of voice.

Make sure that you do not get too caught up in the script. Pay attention to body language and tonality each time you engage with your prospect or client.

THREE DIFFERENT WAYS OF PROCESSING INFORMATION

When building rapport with your prospects and clients, it is also important to understand the ways in which your prospect processes information. Have you ever been in a situation with a prospect where you tried to explain a concept to him several different ways, but he just did not understand the point that you were trying to get across? Typically this happens because we are communicating with him in the way that is most natural for us, not the way in which the other person prefers to communicate.

We find that, in general, people process information three different ways, and when we are in our business development role it is important for us to present information in the way that is easiest for our prospect to understand.

Visuals

The majority of people interpret information visually.

Visuals prefer to have something to look at when you are speaking to them. It is a good idea to bring a brochure or presentation board for a visual person to look at during a meeting because that is the way that he is going to best process the information.

There are several factors that can help you identify a visual person. A visual person often sees the world through pictures and processes information very quickly, so he tends to speak more quickly. Visuals tend to speak fast, move fast, and think fast. They typically are very animated and use gestures while talking. In addition, people who are visuals hate to be interrupted.

If you identify that you are speaking to a visual person, what types of visual aids could you bring into a meeting?

Auditories

When you were in college, law school, or graduate school, did you ever notice that person who would sit in the back of the room and never take notes, but could remember the entire lecture? That person was an auditory, and auditories make up approximately 20 percent of the population.

Auditories view the world in words, sounds, and dialogues. They represent ideas in their mind as conversations, and they tend to speak in even tones and with a steady rhythm. Auditories are more comfortable with people who speak at the same rate that they speak, and they tend to use auditory terms (i.e. "That sounds good," or "I hear what you are saying") in conversations.

Another way to test someone to determine if he is a visual or an auditory is to give him a packet of information when you walk into his office. If he looks through the material, he is more likely a visual, and if he sets the material aside to have a conversation with you, he is more likely to be an auditory.

If you are working with an auditory, the worst thing that you could do to him is make him sit through a PowerPoint presentation. After viewing two slides of the presentation he will stop paying attention, and after three slides he will be ready to throw you out of his office.

Kinesthetics

The last modality that a prospect might perceive the world through is as a kinesthetic. Approximately 25 percent of the population views the world through a kinesthetic lens.

Kinesthetics are influenced by how they feel about their reality. They make judgments on the basis of their inner feelings of comfort or discomfort. Kinesthetics tend to have low-pitched voices and speak at a slow pace. Kinesthetics are the prospects who like to understand exactly how everything works together. Often, providing case studies and detailed outlines is the way to make kinesthetics more comfortable with you.

THE TOWER OF BABEL

Many times you will be in a situation where you are presenting to multiple people at the same time.

When presenting to a group of people, the best strategy is to implement all three styles into your presentation. You should have visual aids for the visuals, have conversations for the auditories, and provide case studies for the kinesthetics.

When we provide training sessions for our clients, we incorporate handouts and PowerPoints for the visuals and provide conversation and debate for the auditories, and our clients participate in role-playing to help show the kinesthetics how to implement the concepts that we teach.

With advances in technology, it has become more and more difficult to get in touch with our clients and prospects. Many times our clients will complain to us because they reach out to their prospects multiple times and they cannot seem to connect with them.

Before the end of the first meeting, we always ask our prospects about their preferred method of communication. We find that some prospects prefer to talk on the phone, some prefer to meet in person, some prefer to email, and others prefer to text. In addition, for ongoing relationships, we ask how often they would like to communicate, what day of the week is easier for them to talk, and even what time of day is typically least busy for them. We find that some people prefer regular communication, and others prefer to speak only when there is a need. Once our prospects and clients tell us how they prefer to communicate, we make a note in their file and make sure to communicate with them in the way that *they* prefer.

Once you focus on ways that you can relate to your prospect and make the meeting about him, you will find that your prospects will open up to you and share more information. For some of you, once you build strong rapport up front, your prospects will tell you exactly what they need in order to do business with you.

You will find that once you focus on making the prospect

comfortable, the next six steps of the business development process will be much easier for you.

In the next chapter we will talk about the Up-Front Contract Step.

Recap: Bonding and Rapport

- Your first and most important job is to make sure the prospect is comfortable.
- Attire, body language, and vocal cues are more important than the words we use.
- Visuals prefer to have something to look at when you are speaking to them.
- Auditories view the world in words, sounds, and dialogues.
- Kinesthetics are strongly influenced by how they feel about their reality.
- You need to make the discussion about the other person!

CHAPTER EIGHTEEN

The Up-Front Contract

*"I like to wing it at the beginning of a
meeting. Why is that a bad thing?"*

Think back to some of the meetings you may have had with
potential clients in the past that did not end up turning into
business. What were some of the roadblocks that surfaced?

Did you ever prepare for a one-hour meeting, only to be cut off
halfway into it? Or did the opposite ever happen where you were
expecting an initial 30-minute meeting, but your prospect was hoping
to get two hours of free consulting? Did you ever have a meeting that
you thought went well, but afterwards you were unclear about when
and how to take the next steps? Maybe you had a first meeting that
ended with the words, "Let us think it over."

The Up-Front Contract Step is a tool to ensure that you never
encounter those situations again.

Up-Front Contract

The second compartment of the Sandler Submarine is the Up-Front
Contract Step. An up-front contract is an agenda to ensure that we are
on the same page as our prospect at all times. An up-front contract will
also help you more quickly qualify or disqualify each opportunity.

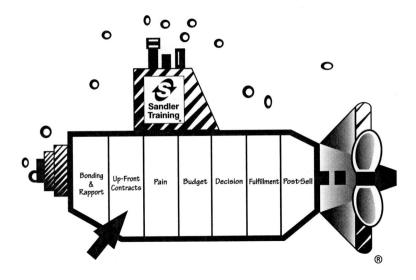

The goal for the Up-Front Contract Step is to obtain clear next steps for what will occur after your meeting. An up-front contract will also help you to differentiate yourself from your competitors right from the beginning and provide you with a technique to make your prospects feel more comfortable and in control, while allowing you to retain control of the meeting.

Often your prospects are guarded before meeting with you for the first time for a variety of reasons. Some of your prospect's biggest fears include:

- He is afraid you will waste his time.
- He is concerned that you will not understand his business.
- He is concerned that he will get a "hard sell" at the end of the meeting.

Thank You

The first component of the Up-Front Contract Step is a simple "thank you." You want to show your appreciation for either the prospect coming to meet with you at your office, or for the prospect inviting you into his office.

This part of the Up-Front Contract Step only takes 30 seconds to complete, but there are one or two nuances that you need to incorporate. First, you want to be on equal footing with the person with whom you are meeting.

Often, especially if you are meeting with a senior contact in the target organization, you may make the mistake of putting the prospect on a pedestal. We have seen professionals tell the person with whom they are meeting that they are grateful for the appointment, they know how important or busy this person is, they are happy with just a few minutes of his time, and so on. This kind of remark immediately puts you in a subservient position to your prospect, and as the business development process progresses, the prospect may not respect you or value your time.

During the meeting, you must keep in mind that you are the expert at what you do. You have valuable expertise to provide your prospect, regardless of his title or position.

Set the Clock

During the initial phone call, you should establish the objective of the meeting, the outcome you and your prospect will be working toward, and each person's role in achieving that outcome. Last but not least, you should agree to the time allotted for the meeting. A mutually-agreed-to agenda keeps the meeting focused and on track. Once you show up, you should review all of these elements of the Up-Front Contract Step to make sure that it is still intact.

A mutual understanding of the time allotted for the meeting is particularly important. We have worked with a number of attorneys and accountants who became frustrated because a prospect would try to take up to two hours of their time in an attempt to get as much free consulting as possible in a first meeting. These professionals were struggling to find ways to limit that free consulting. The answer: set and honor clear up-front contracts!

We have also worked with consultants, architects, and engineers who were frustrated because a potential client would only give them 30 minutes for a first meeting, and they felt like they could not fully understand their prospect's needs in that amount of time.

You must get an agreement on the length of the initial meeting during the phone call when the meeting is scheduled. If your prospect cannot give you enough time to meet, then change the date/time of the appointment so that you will have enough time to properly qualify or disqualify the opportunity.

The Prospect's Agenda

After we have covered the basics, the next step is to ask the prospect for his agenda. It is vital that we find out why the prospect agreed to take a meeting with us, and we need to find out what objectives the prospect was hoping to accomplish during the course of the meeting.

Although this step may seem obvious to some, we find that too often professionals assume they know why the prospect has agreed to meet with them, and they start to "pitch" the prospect after the first few minutes. Unfortunately, most of us are not very good mind readers. In addition, your prospect will feel invested in the meeting if he believes that the agenda has been set around his needs.

When someone starts to pitch a prospect before he learns what the prospect is really looking for, there is a good chance that he will guess incorrectly. The prospect will lose interest if you start presenting on a topic that seems irrelevant, or if your perspective is one with which he disagrees.

We have found that a big fear prospects have is that their time will be wasted. If you start presenting on a topic the prospect is not really interested in, he is likely to tune out the message.

When we discuss this concept in our training sessions, we often hear chuckles from the professionals who are working for large firms. Often those firms go into a big meeting with a "pitch book" that focuses, not on the needs of the prospect, but on what makes the firm great and the various reasons the prospect should work with them. Your prospects have their own reasons for choosing with whom they will work. If your pitch book does not address them and their issues, they will not be calling you back. It really is that simple.

Asking for your prospect's agenda will allow you to focus on his problems. If he has several issues that he would like to discuss, have him prioritize which of those issues he believes is the most important. Once you allow the prospect to share what he believes is his most important issue, you can then begin to address his concerns.

CASE IN POINT

One of our clients, Mike, was a consultant to the financial services industry. Mike told us that before he started working with us, he would work out a pitch for a meeting, and as soon as he arrived to his initial meeting, he would begin to present.

After Mike learned about the Up-Front Contract Step, he started asking his prospects what they were hoping he could show them and how they hoped he could help them. Mike said that his prospects would tell him exactly what they needed to see and hear from him during the course of the meeting.

Mike's closing ratio increased dramatically, and he said that it had never, in his entire career, been so quick or so easy to close business.

Asking a Question About Asking Questions

After you get the prospect to share his agenda, you should share what you were hoping to cover in the meeting. The most important idea to keep in mind when sharing your agenda is that you want to *ask the prospect's permission to ask questions during the course of the meeting.*

Often, we will hear our clients use statements like, "Everyone we meet with has different issues," or "I want to make sure I understand everything that you are looking for, so would you mind if I asked some specific questions during the course of the meeting?"

In our 20-plus years of consulting, we have never heard anyone claim that his prospect would not be OK answering a few questions.

Asking permission to ask questions will change the paradigm of a meeting from you making a presentation for your prospect, to you having a conversation with your prospect. In addition, the prospect will feel flattered because he will understand that you are interested in solving his problems, not in just making a presentation.

Finally, the permission to ask questions will allow you to utilize a tactic called "Reversing," a powerful questioning technique you will learn more about in the next chapter.

Just Say "No"

The next piece of the Up-Front Contract Step is the most important, but it will also be the piece that will, at first, be the most uncomfortable for you to use. We want you to set the expectation with your prospects that, by the end of the meeting, they will need to make a decision.

We want you to strongly encourage your prospects, if they are not interested in your services, and if they do not believe that there is a good fit between what they are looking for and what you have to offer, to please tell you *no.*

In addition, we want you to ask the prospects if they would be comfortable if you tell them *no* should you determine that you were not the best fit for them and cannot help them with their problems.

For some, it might sound counterintuitive to encourage our prospect to tell us *no*. But with the Sandler approach, if someone is not going to do business with us, we want to uncover that fact in the first meeting rather than providing free consulting, sitting through several meetings, and then finding out the answer is *no*. In our experience, we have never had a prospect who was interested in our services say *no* because we gave them permission to do so. In addition, many of our clients have reported that their prospects gave them more respect after they offered to make it easy for them to say *no*.

This piece of the Up-Front Contract Step will help to differentiate you from your competitors in the first part of the first meeting.

Tell Me That You Want Me

We also urge you to encourage your prospects to tell you if they would like to move forward at the end of the first meeting. Typically, our clients will say something like, "If this looks like it might be a fit, can we take the last five minutes of the meeting to discuss the next steps?" A *yes* does not mean that someone will agree to sign a contract at the end of the first meeting; it just means that he will agree to discuss the next steps before the meeting is over.

By sharing with the prospect that it is OK to say *no*, and that we need to agree upon next steps if he is interested, you will find that your prospect engages with you more during the meeting. Once the prospect realizes that a decision will need to be made at the end of the meeting, he will ask more questions and be more involved in the process.

Once you master the components of the Up-Front Contract Step, you will find that you are able to move into the next compartment of the submarine, Pain, with ease. In addition, once you implement an up-front contract, you will shorten your selling cycle, and your follow up with prospects and clients will take less effort.

In the next chapter we will talk about Pain and how to identify it.

Recap: Key Points of the Up-Front Contract Step

- Thank you
- Time
- Prospect's Agenda
- Our Agenda
- Give the prospect permission to say *no* if there is not a fit
- Ask the prospect for permission to discuss the next steps towards the end of the meeting if he would like to move forward

CHAPTER NINETEEN

Pain

"What is pain, anyway?"

We find that one of the biggest mistakes professionals make when meeting with potential clients is that they assume they know *what* their prospects are looking for, and they assume they know the reasons *why* their prospect is going to make a decision.

We have known many professionals who are so confident in both their skills and their assumptions as to what the prospect is looking for, that they believe the only way to close a deal is to prove their expertise at the beginning of the first meeting. We call this "Show Up and Throw Up," or "Premature Presentation Syndrome."

We worked with a large actuary firm that was proud of the presentations they would put together for a first meeting with a prospective client. The firm would include bios of everyone in the firm, a list of projects that they had completed, and their ideas for the client's project. Initially, this firm hired us because they could not understand why they were not closing more deals based on their detailed and well-prepared presentations. Their closing percentage was about 15 percent.

Their entire presentation would be developed *before* making sure they understood exactly what their prospect was looking for and the reasons why their prospects were in the market for a new firm.

After spending several hours discussing the low closing percentage, this firm discovered that it was not in their best interest to present information before finding out the needs and wants of their prospect. In chapter sixteen, we discussed many reasons why it may not be in your best interests, or the prospect's best interests, to provide free consulting at the beginning of the meeting.

UNCOVERING PAIN

Before making any kind of presentation, you must identify the areas where there is a gap between where the prospect is and where he wants to be. We call this "Pain." You must discover how these areas of need impact the prospect, and then determine whether your services can bridge the gap.

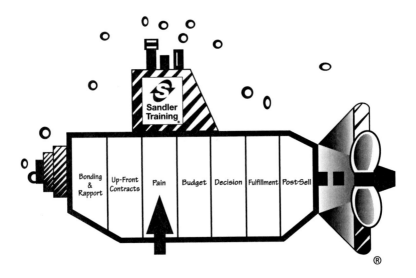

The most effective and the most client-friendly way to determine if you can help a prospect is by using your expertise to ask the right questions when you are meeting with your prospective client for the first time.

If you review the Up-Front Contract Step chapter (chapter eighteen), you will see that one of the parts of the Up-Front Contract Step is to ask your prospect for his agenda. Asking the prospect for his agenda is the best way to initiate the pain process. Two of the best questions that you can ask someone early in the meeting is, "What were you hoping to get from this meeting," or "How were you hoping I was going to help you?"

Once your prospect answers those initial questions, you will have a good idea of where you should start the conversation. If the prospect does not answer your question, or if he is not sure how you can help, the 30-second commercial can be a great tool to jumpstart the pain conversation. After you utilize an extended version of your 30-second commercial, you can ask your prospect which of those issues or pains he would like to discuss, or you can ask him if there was another problem that he was hoping you could help him resolve.

It is our experience that once prospects have agreed to meet with you, they are willing to share with you what their agenda is for that meeting.

Why Ask "Why"?

Why do we ask questions at the beginning of the meeting if we believe that we know what our prospect's issues are, and how we think we can help?

Have you ever had a meeting with a salesperson or advisor that you have never met before? You were anxious to have an in-depth conversation about some business or personal challenges that you had been facing, and you hoped that this person could help you overcome these challenges. How would you feel if, at the beginning of that meeting, before asking a single question, that person said, "I understand all of your challenges, and I've got the perfect solution for you"?

What are the chances that this person would be able to read your mind and know exactly what you need? Why do we think we can assume that we know what our clients or prospects want or need before an initial conversation? In addition, how many of your competitors are leading with their expertise and their solutions before they learn about the prospect's challenges from the prospect's perspective?

First Things First

If you meet with someone and he shares that there are two or three different things that he would like to cover, we suggest that you ask your prospect which of those issues are the most important to him, and where he would like to start the conversation. You may disagree with your prospect about which issue is the most important, but if you tell your prospect he should be focusing in a different area first, the prospect may believe that you do not understand him or his issues.

In our experience, your prospects will have problems that fall into two different categories.

The first category is an issue that falls directly into your area of expertise. In this case, prospects know they will need to hire somebody with expertise in that specific area to help them resolve their problem. For example, if an employer has just been sued by a former employee, the employer knows he will need to get an employment attorney with experience in litigation to help him resolve the matter.

The second category is when a prospect is looking to change providers. In this case, the prospect might be unhappy with one of your competitors, and he is looking to find someone new. Many of the mid-sized accounting firms and law firms that we help often get calls from companies that are working with larger firms, but are not happy with the services they are receiving. Sometimes the prospective client is unhappy because he does not believe he is getting the attention of the partners of his current firm, he does not see the value that he is getting for the premium fee he is paying, or he might be unhappy because there is no consistency with the professionals who are providing the work. Any of these pains may be enough for someone to change providers.

It is your job to ask clarifying questions to determine how your prospect believes these issues are impacting him, and to ask him how he would prefer to work with a new provider.

WHAT'S THE IMPACT?

Once you uncover a problem that your prospect is experiencing, it is your job to utilize your expertise to question your prospect as to what the impact to him could be if that problem is not resolved.

In our experience, at the beginning of the conversation, your prospect will talk about the symptoms of the overall problem (we call these pain indicators), rather than discussing the impact that the problem could have on either his organization or on him personally. Some reasons your prospect might do this are that he either does not understand what the larger issue is, or he has never dealt with that specific problem before. Other times your prospect may try to minimize his issue because he thinks that if he talks about the impact of his problems, you will charge him more money to fix it.

CASE IN POINT

David, an international tax attorney, helps US-based businesses when they open offices in other countries, and he sometimes helps businesses from other countries who want to open offices in the United States. Some of the companies David works with have never opened international offices, and they do not realize all the negative implications of not setting things up in the correct way at the beginning of the process. David often needs to ask a lot of questions and share third-party stories before his prospects understand what their true pain could be if they do not work with the right attorney.

The problems you uncover can have impacts in any number of areas. Here is an overview of some of the most common impact areas.

Financial Impact

The first impact that a prospect's problems could have is that his problems could cost money. For instance, a consultant may talk to a company and learn that the company is missing out on new business opportunities and could be leaving revenue on the table. A different company may find that it might be able to save money if it were to do things a little differently.

CASE IN POINT

A client of ours, Drew, is a consultant in the telecom industry. Drew's main job is to find cost savings for his clients. Drew typically works with CFOs of companies and can save those companies hundreds of thousands of dollars, without requiring them to change services or providers. As Drew asks his clients questions, he might be able to identify roughly how much money they are losing. By asking the correct questions, he can figure out how the company can save money without disrupting the current service. In addition, Drew can help companies discover new revenue sources that might provide the company with funding needed to spend on other projects.

Time Impact

The next type of challenge that might cause pain for one of your prospects is if he is dealing with an issue or problem that is taking up too much of his time internally.

CASE IN POINT

Todd owns a specialized IT services company. Many times Todd will talk with prospects who are frustrated because they are spending too much time, internally, trying to complete a project that could move the business forward. The company will often have employees who have the technical ability to complete the project, but they just do not have the time to take on additional work.

Todd will often show a client how his company can free up a prospect's employees to complete essential tasks and make the entire department more efficient.

Pain Questions

Tell me more about that...

**Can you be more specific?
Give me an example.**

**How long has that
been a problem?**

**What have you tried
to do about that?**

And did that work?

**How much do
you think that
has cost you?**

**How do you feel
about that?**

**Have you given
up trying to
deal with the
problem?**

Sandler*works!*

In the Pain Compartment of the Submarine, it is important to identify one pain, then move from the top of the Sandler Pain Funnel® (pain indicators) through the bottom of the Pain Funnel (impact of time, money, and liability) on that one issue. If it is possible, quantify the impact that the first pain is having on the prospect before moving to the second pain.

In an ideal world, we want you to identify two to four pains that the prospect is experiencing and quantify the impact of each of those pains on the organization, as well as its impact on the individual.

Once you have identified the pain, the next step in the Sandler Submarine, the Budget Step, will be much easier to complete if you have also taken the time to quantify that pain.

In the next chapter, we will explore the Budget Compartment of the Sandler Submarine.

Recap: Sample Pain Questions-

- What recent example of that comes to mind?
- How long has that been a problem?
- What have you tried in the past to fix the problem?
- What's worked for you, and what hasn't?
- Why do you think you got the results you did?
- Is it getting worse or better, and how fast?
- How much do you figure that has cost you?
- What is the most recent action you have taken to correct it?
- If you could wave a magic wand in this situation, what would it do?
- What personal distress is this causing you?
- How much are you willing to invest to solve the problem?
- How do you see me helping you?

CHAPTER TWENTY

Budget

"If I ask about money, I'll scare them off."

After you have identified your prospects' pain, it is important to uncover the budget — the time, money, and other resources — they have set aside for solving their problems.

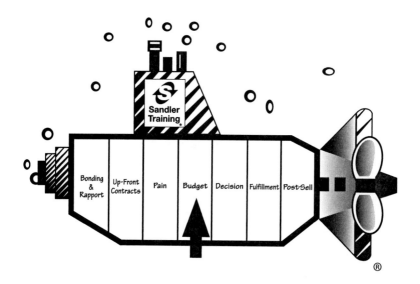

Over the years, we have spoken with many professional service firms that do not address the budget until the end of the business development process. When the budget is not identified early in the process, it can lead to wasted time later, after you have already put together a proposal or presentation for someone who either cannot afford or does not see value in your services.

We have seen firms leave money on the table because they pitched a minimal level of service, believing the prospect did not have much of a budget. They found out later that their prospect could have allocated a larger budget and received appropriate services that would have been a much better fit for solving his problems.

On the other end of the spectrum, we have met architects who spent hours putting together great concepts and beautiful designs, only to find out that their services were triple or even quadruple what their prospect could afford to pay.

We have seen law firms run into problems with their clients in litigation matters because their prospect did not understand how much the cost of litigation might be and was angry and upset upon receiving his first bill because expectations were not properly set in advance.

In some cases, not being clear about budget can ruin a relationship with your client or prospect, even if you have provided him with great service.

THE PRICE OF PAIN

The services you are providing, and the client's familiarity with purchasing your services, will all have an impact on the Budget Step. Many professionals forget or are unaware that the key piece of the Budget Step is to understand the importance of tying the budget back to your prospect's pain.

Did you quantify the pain (cost of your prospect's problems) before you moved from the Pain Step to the Budget Step? Does your prospect understand what the cost could be if he does not receive the proper services, or the liability that he may be open to if those services are not performed correctly? Is your prospect aware of the cost and impact to his organization, or to him personally, if the project is delayed or not serviced properly?

MANAGING EXPECTATIONS

Another critical concept in the Budget Step is managing the expectations of your clients.

CASE IN POINT

One of our law firm clients, Andre, came to us because he was having a collections issue with some of his clients. Andre believed he was doing good work for his clients, but then the clients would bitterly complain because the bills were larger than they had expected.

When we asked Andre to tell us about the budget conversations he was having with his clients, he responded that he shared his hourly rates up front, and that his clients agreed to those hourly rates. When we asked him about the expectations that were set with the client about the approximate cost for litigation, he said that his firm could not possibly quote a price because there were too many variables that were outside of his control.

We then asked him if, in his experience, he had an idea of what the high end and low end cost of litigation could be. He said that he could take an educated guess, and he could give his clients parameters of their potential cost based on the complexity of the case and the mindset of the opposing attorney. When we asked him if he was sharing that information with his clients, the answer was "No."

We then asked Andre how he would feel if we sent him a bill that was much larger than he expected. He admitted that getting a bill that was larger than he expected would not make him very happy.

At that point, Andre began to realize how his clients must feel when they received large unexpected bills from his firm. Once he took a walk in his client's shoes, he realized the importance of setting and managing the budget expectations with his clients.

As Andre began to put this into practice by properly setting expectations with his clients, the collections issues went away and his clients were happy to regularly engage his services.

BUDGET QUESTIONS

There are three primary questions that need to be answered in the Budget Compartment of the submarine. The first issue is to determine whether your potential client is willing to make any investment to solve his problems.

In many cases, the prospect will only be willing to move forward if there is not much cost and not much work involved in fixing the problem. If the prospect is not willing to make an investment to fix the problem, it is important to uncover that issue as early in the process as possible, so that you do not fall into the trap of providing free consulting for an unqualified prospect.

CASE IN POINT

We had a client, named Bruce, who was an intellectual property attorney. Bruce worked with individuals and organizations who had invented a product or new service, and Bruce's job was to protect that person's idea so that it would not be stolen.

Many times individuals would come to Bruce with an idea, but they did not understand the cost or time commitment involved in securing a new patent. Initially, when Bruce came to us, he was very frustrated because he would spend hours doing research for potential clients and providing free consulting, only to find that those individuals were not willing, or sometimes not able, to pay for the cost of his services.

Once we started working with Bruce, he began asking qualifying questions about his prospects' budget over the phone, before meeting with them for the initial consult. Bruce found that he would disqualify many prospects in his initial phone conversations rather than wasting time meeting with unqualified prospects. However, when Bruce met with the pre-qualified prospects, the success rate of those initial meetings jumped to a closing rate in excess of 75 percent.

How Much?

The second question of the Budget Compartment is to uncover the amount of money a prospect is willing to invest in order to solve his problems. This step will look different for each of you, depending on your business and the types of clients you serve. For some prospects, you may need to set expectations of the services you can provide at different budget levels and work together with your client to determine how much he is willing or able to spend.

Unfortunately, very few of our prospects will openly and honestly answer when we ask, "What is your budget?" But there are several techniques you can utilize to uncover the truth.

Bracketing

The first tactic our clients find helpful when trying to uncover their prospect's budget is called "bracketing."

Bracketing is a tactic whereby you give the prospect a pricing range for your solution within which the investment is likely to fall, without getting pinned down to a specific price. So if you want to charge $10,000 for your solution, but you have no idea how the prospect is going to respond to that price, you might say, "Typically, working with clients in your industry, we find that the investment for this solution runs between $9,000 and $14,000. Can you be comfortable within that range?"

Telling Tales

Another very successful tactic that our clients utilize is telling third-party stories about solutions they have provided for clients in the past.

In this tactic, the prospect is given a high end example of a solution that you have previously provided, a mid-range solution, and a low end solution. The prospect is then asked which type of solution makes the most sense for his situation.

This tactic accomplishes two things. First, it can give your prospect a good idea of the different solutions you can provide within various budget levels. Second, it can provide you with additional credibility because your prospect will discover that you have a lot of experience solving problems like his.

Past Experience

Finally, it might make sense to ask your prospect if he has utilized services similar to yours or tried to solve a similar problem in the past. If the answer to that question is *yes*, your next question should be, "What did you invest to fix that problem?"

His answer to this question will help you determine if you are speaking with a qualified prospect and give you an idea of where your fee needs to be to win the client.

COST VERSUS VALUE

Another concept that is important in the Budget Step is the idea of cost versus value.

CASE IN POINT

Bill is an engineer. One of the services that Bill's firm provides is building handicapped ramps in a major city. Bill was talking to a contractor about building the ramps, and the contractor asked Bill about his rates. When Bill shared his rates, the contractor said that Bill's rates were too high. Bill asked the contractor why he was asking for quotes from another engineer since this project had been running for a long time. The contractor shared with Bill that the ramps were not being constructed correctly, his original engineer was missing deadlines, and some of the ramps needed to be rebuilt.

Bill asked the contractor if it would have been less expensive to use the right engineer the first time instead of having ramps rebuilt and projects delayed. That contractor began to realize that the cheapest price is not always the best value, and Bill ultimately won the work.

WHAT'S IN THEIR WALLET?

The final question to be answered in the Budget Step is to find out whether your prospect is willing and able to make the investment to fix his problem.

You might find that someone is very interested in working with you, but he just does not have the budget to start the project. You might also find that the person with whom you are speaking would like to move forward, but someone else in his organization controls the financial decisions.

As part of the qualification process, you must determine if the person you are meeting with has the ability to spend the money.

In the next chapter, we will learn about the Decision Compartment of the Sandler Submarine.

Recap: Budget

- Bracketing
- Third-party stories
- Previous history
- Questions you should answer in the Budget Step
  - Is the prospect willing to make an investment?
  - How much is the prospect willing to invest?
  - Is the prospect able to make an investment?

CHAPTER TWENTY-ONE

Decision

"Why do I need to worry about this?"

T he next compartment in the Sandler Submarine is called the
Decision Step.
Decision is the step that is most often overlooked in the
qualifying process. This is unfortunate, because this is the step that

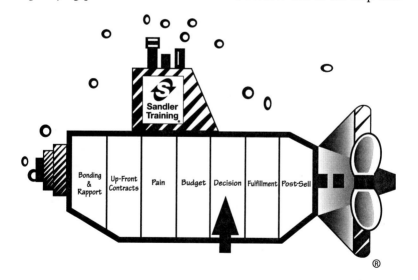

is most important in determining whether you will be able to move forward with the opportunity!

Here, you want to know how the prospect will make the decision. The answers that you receive in this part of the submarine will help you determine how much sense it really makes to move forward with this opportunity. These answers will also help guide you as to how you should proceed with your next steps.

Let us take a look at what can happen if you do not qualify your opportunity by clarifying how your prospect is going to make a decision.

CASE IN POINT

Carl was a partner in the audit department of a mid-sized regional accounting firm. One of the target markets for this accounting firm is non-profits. Carl was able to secure an appointment with a large non-profit, and his two meetings with the executive director went very well. Carl had identified several areas where his firm could help this non-profit, and his firm was also going to be able to provide services that the incumbent accounting firm could not provide.

Carl heard from the executive director that there was no question that he was winning the work. He just needed to provide a detailed proposal and a contract. It took Carl's firm about one week (about 60 hours' worth of work) to get the proposal and contract to the non-profit. Carl provided good follow up and called to make sure that the non-profit received the proposal and contract. The executive director said that everything "looked good" and that Carl could expect to receive a signed contract and retainer check within the week.

One week went by and Carl had not received the contract. Carl followed up with the executive director several times over the next few weeks, and the executive director (who had been very responsive throughout the entire process) would not return his phone calls. After three weeks and several attempted contacts, Carl received an email from the executive director stating that the non-profit had decided to stay with the incumbent firm.

This was a fresh wound for Carl. Carl simply could not believe that he had not gotten the business, and he was angry and disappointed that the non-profit stayed with the incumbent firm.

At our suggestion, Carl called and left a message for the executive director asking if he could have an "off-the-record" conversation to find out why they lost the business, so that his firm could do better in the future. The executive director returned Carl's call.

During the course of the conversation, Carl found out that several members of this non-profit's board of directors were personal friends with the managing partner of the incumbent accounting firm, and those personal relationships were the reason that the non-profit stayed with their incumbent firm. In fact, the incumbent was incorporating many of the ideas in Carl's proposal for the upcoming year.

Carl was caught completely off guard because the executive director never shared with him that the board of directors was making the decision. He assumed that because he was talking with the executive director, and she presented herself as the decision maker, that he was talking to the right person.

Because Carl did not properly identify the decision-making process for his prospect, he provided free consulting and invested countless hours of his firm's time into an opportunity that he never had a chance of closing.

ASK THE RIGHT QUESTIONS

In the Decision Step of the qualifying process, you need to ask all of the questions that a good journalist would ask when covering a news story.

Who?

The most important information to uncover is *Who* is making the decision. Is the person to whom you are speaking part of the decision-making process, or is he simply gathering information for someone else? Does the person with whom you are speaking have the authority to approve a decision, or does he only have the authority to say *no*? If this person is making the decision, is there anyone else who will help him to make that decision?

How?

The next question we need to have answered in the decision-making process is *How* the decision being made.

Is one person making the decision, or is a committee involved? If a decision is being made for a large organization, how many different departments need to sign off on the decision? Does a procurement department need to sign off on the decision? If you are going after bid work or work with non-profits, are they required to obtain a certain number of bids? Will the presentations take place via proposal or in person with a presentation, or will a site visit be involved? Is there going to be an RFP or RFQ process, and how closely is the prospect sticking to that process?

CASE IN POINT

Terry is a corporate attorney who called us because she received a request for a proposal for a very attractive and high profile project in her city. Terry and her firm had successfully worked on several projects that were similar to this project, and she thought that it would be a good opportunity for her firm. As Terry read through the request, she realized that a proper response to the proposal would be over 100 pages long and take weeks to complete. Terry asked us if she should pursue the opportunity.

At our suggestion, Terry called the contact for the project to ask how many other firms were receiving this RFP. Terry was told that over 100 firms received the RFP, and a response was required within two weeks. Terry checked with us to see what she should do. Based on our recommendation, Terry conducted some research to find out who was responsible for making the decision. We also suggested that Terry reach out to the clients to whom she had provided similar work, and those clients wrote her glowing recommendations on their company letterhead. Terry then overnighted those letters to the decision maker with a cover letter asking if this organization was interested in having a similar experience with her law firm.

The decision maker from this organization called Terry and told her not to worry about the RFP, as they had decided to award the work to her firm.

After Terry received the work, she asked why the organization did not make her go through the RFP process. Terry was told that the RFP was designed to find firms who claimed they could provide the right services, but Terry's letters proved that she had already successfully provided those services to other organizations. In fact, the decision maker knew one of the people who wrote a letter for Terry and called him.

By the way, that organization received over 50 responses to the RFP, and those responses were never even read.

Where?

The next important piece of information to uncover is *Where* the decision is being made.

For those of you who are targeting national or global accounts, you need to determine if decisions can be made out of the local office, or if someone in a corporate office needs to make the ultimate decision. The answers to those questions may determine whether or not you proceed with the opportunity, and what steps you will take to move the opportunity to the next step.

What?

The next journalism question that we need to ask is *What* decision is going to be made.

Is the prospect looking for a major change, or is he looking to test the waters? Does he want a full project or a pilot program? When a decision is made, what exactly is being decided?

Why?

The next question is one of the most important questions, and a question that should have been partially or mostly uncovered in the Pain Step. We need to uncover *Why* the prospect is looking to make a decision.

If he has been working with someone else, why is he looking to make a change now? If the problem you were brought in to fix has been festering for a long period of time, why is he looking to fix it now? In our experience, it is more difficult to get someone to make a decision if he has been putting up with the problem for a long time (or an incumbent who is not providing great work), versus someone who has just begun to experience challenges.

Often, professionals will make the mistake of assuming they know the reasons someone is making a decision rather than getting their prospect to express his reasons during the qualification process. As you are asking questions about why your prospect is making a decision, you may want to refer back to the pain that you uncovered in the Pain Step — and you might want to quantify for your prospect the cost of those pains.

When?

The last question that we need to ask in the Decision Step is *When* the decision is going to be made. We also need to understand when the prospect was hoping to get started, and when he was hoping to have a resolution.

For some, you may find out that the prospect is not looking to make a decision in the near future, and that information may impact the way in which you will move forward. For many of the architects and builders that we work with, their clients do not have much experience with developing projects, and they may have unrealistic expectations about the length of time it takes to get things like permits and licenses approved. You may need to spend some time in the Decision Step managing expectations.

In addition, if you find that your prospect is under a time constraint to get something accomplished, you will be more likely to have your prospects make a quick decision.

Once you obtain the answers to the questions in the Decision Step, you can make an informed decision about whether or not it makes sense to move forward in the process. If you are uncomfortable about how the decision is being made (or you think that your prospect is just fishing for free consulting) there is no law that says you must make a presentation.

> The Sandler Selling System is used to help you *qualify* **or** *disqualify* opportunities. If the prospect is not qualified, do not provide free consulting.

If the prospect is qualified, you will move to the next compartment of the Sandler Submarine.

In the next chapter, you will learn about the Fulfillment Step.

Recap: Questions about the Decision
- Who?
- Who else?
- How?
- Where?
- What?
- Why?
- When?

CHAPTER TWENTY-TWO

Fulfillment

*"All I can do is put together my best proposal,
and then wait for them to call me back."*

O nce you have qualified your opportunity by uncovering
your prospect's pain, made sure that your prospect has a
budget and is willing to invest that budget, and uncovered

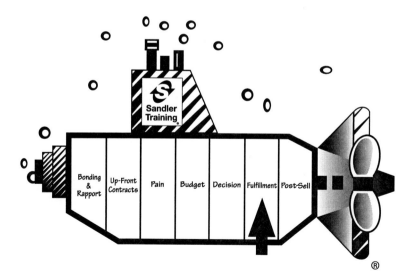

the process that the prospect will be using to make his decision, it is time for the next compartment of the Sandler Submarine — the Fulfillment Step.

In the Fulfillment Step, there are two big picture events that are about to take place. First, you are finally going to present your ideas and expertise to your prospect. Second, the prospect will be required to make a decision.

In the Fulfillment Step, we are going to demonstrate to our prospect how our solutions will fix his problems.

The Fulfillment Step will look different based on the industry and the type of prospect.

Take the Deal

For some attorneys and accountants, the Fulfillment Step may actually take place in the initial meeting. For attorneys and accountants who do a very good job uncovering pain with a small opportunity, there may not be a need to do a true Fulfillment Step. If your client believes that you can help because you did a thorough job uncovering his issues in the Pain Step, you may not be required to make a large presentation.

Some professionals make a major mistake in believing they must do a presentation. They will continue to talk even after the prospect has indicated he is ready to work with them. At that point, the only thing the professional can accomplish is to talk his way out of winning new business.

Most of us have heard of someone talking his way out of the business by continuing to present even though the prospect was ready to make a decision. Our guess is that you have never heard of someone listening his way out of the business!

The first rule of business is to close the business and take the money. If the decision makers are ready to make a commitment, let them commit! Do not worry. Your prospect will not ask for a discount because you did not provide a presentation.

One Size Fits All — Not

For many of the architects and engineers that we work with, the Fulfillment Step is much more involved. Often, for these professionals, the Fulfillment Step will consist of days or weeks of putting a proposal together. Once the proposal is completed, there may be several rounds of meetings and presentations before a decision is made.

The components of the Fulfillment Step are equally applicable to opportunities that close in one meeting as they are to longer selling cycles, you just need to modify the steps based on the ways that your opportunities take place.

It also helps to work with a coach to strategize your larger business development opportunities.

Up-Front Contract

When you schedule your Fulfillment Step presentation, you will want to establish another up-front contract, just as you did for the first meeting. Be sure to incorporate the different roles and responsibilities of everyone involved, as well as the expectations/outcomes (e.g., a *yes* or *no* decision) you both agree will arise from the discussion.

Review the contract before you begin your presentation. If any of the elements have changed, and the change would prevent you from achieving the agreed-upon outcome, you may have to reschedule your presentation.

As we hope you have gathered by now, these contracts are essential throughout the business development process, just as good rapport with the prospect is essential. An up-front contract is particularly important right now. Before making your presentation, we want you to ask your prospect what happens if he likes the presentation/proposal, and what the next steps will be.

There can be challenges in turning your prospect into a client if your prospect cannot (or will not) tell you what will take place if he likes your presentation. If you get the feeling that you are just getting shopped around, you are certainly not required to provide a presentation.

Remember — you only make a presentation if the prospect qualifies to get one!

CASE IN POINT

We worked with an architectural firm that had been badly burned by a prospect who would not give them a commitment before the Fulfillment Step. The architect firm was bidding on building a new church. After their presentation (and many, many follow-up calls), they were told that their design did not get selected.

Two years later, those architects drove by the church, which looked exactly like their design, but they knew that it was not their firm that won the bid.

These architects did a lot of free consulting for another firm that not only won the bid, but also copied their design!

Pain Review

After you set a new up-front contract, the next step is to review which pains were uncovered in the Pain Step. If the presentation is happening after the initial meeting, it is important to remind your prospect about the problems that you uncovered in the Pain Step. In an ideal world, you will have your prospect restate his problems to you.

Once the prospect has restated his problems, we want to ask the prospect which of the problems he views as the most crucial. It is key to start the presentation by addressing the problem your prospect feels is the most important. If you disagree with the prospect about what his most important problem is, he will believe that you do not really understand his issues. In your presentation, it is important to allow your prospect to lead in terms of what he would like to address first.

A major mistake we have seen firms make in the past is that they will put together a presentation or pitch, and that presentation will be focused on the strength of their firm instead of their prospect's problems.

Several things happen when we pitch ourselves instead of focusing on our prospect's problems. First, your prospect will feel like you have not listened to him and that you do not understand his problems. Next, you will come across as being very similar to the rest of your competitors. Finally, you may end up spending very little time addressing what the prospect perceives as his most pressing issues.

After you allow the prospect to prioritize his pains, address the prospect's most important issue first. After you have completely addressed the ways you will help solve that initial problem, ask your prospect if he is completely satisfied with your solution. If he is not completely satisfied with your solution, it is your job to ask why he is not satisfied and continue to address that issue.

If you cannot agree on the proper way to address his most important issue, is there any chance you will get his business?

If your prospect is satisfied with your solution to his most important issue, then move to his next issue. After you have finished addressing his next issue, again ask if he is completely satisfied.

Repeat this step until you have addressed all of your prospect's issues.

TAKING THE TEMPERATURE

During the Fulfillment Step, you will want to use what we call the Thermometer Technique.

The thermometer technique is used to find out, while still in the presentation meeting, how close the prospect is to making a decision.

The thermometer close sounds like this: "Now that we have addressed all of your issues, can you give me an idea of where you are on a scale of one to ten? A "one" means that you were uncomfortable with how I addressed all of your issues and that I have wasted your time. A "ten" means that you are completely satisfied with how I have addressed your issues, and you are ready to take the next steps we discussed. Can you share with me where you are on that scale?"

Remember that, before you used the thermometer technique, you asked your prospect how comfortable he was as you addressed each individual pain. It is extremely uncommon for someone to say that he is comfortable with each solution, and then to be less than an eight on the scale. Sometimes, you will not get a number, but the prospect will spend the next five to ten minutes explaining what he liked and what he did not like about your presentation or proposal.

This will help you move forward with your prospect.

THE GENTLE CLOSE

Once your prospects say that they are a 10, or they indicate that they are happy with everything, you want to close the business in a professional manner.

A great question to ask once your prospects indicate that they are interested is, "What would you like me to do now?" If you hear the prospects tell you to take the specific next steps that equate to "ten," which you identified earlier on in the discussion, then you have just closed the sale. If you hear anything other than that, you missed a step.

Notice that, while this closing approach is direct and unambiguous, it is the exact opposite of the "hard sell" close that most selling systems advocate. We do not want to do a hard sell because it is not professional, and it may give your prospects buyer's remorse, causing them to back out of the deal after they have agreed to work with you.

In the next chapter, you will learn about what happens after the sale: the Post-Sell Step.

Recap: Components of the Fulfilment Step

- Up-front contract
- Pain review
- Thermometer technique

CHAPTER TWENTY-THREE

Post-Sell

*"Sometimes people get cold feet.
There is nothing I can do about that."*

Have you ever left a meeting thinking you have locked up the business with a new client, only to hear a few days later that the prospect has backed out of the deal unexpectedly? Guess what? That did not have to happen.

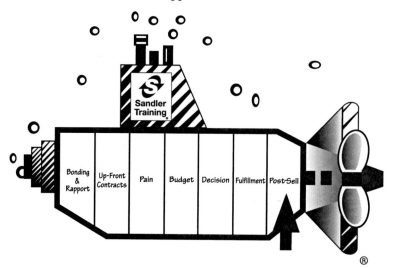

Here is another question: If your prospects do not send you the contract or the initial retainer when they promised it to you, what do you think your chances are of getting a decision maker from that company back on the phone?

To address such issues, the Sandler Submarine has a compartment known as Post-Sell. This compartment is not optional. It is a mandatory part of the professional business development process.

THE UNCLIENT

If you do not perform a good Post-Sell Step, you are needlessly increasing the chance that your prospects may change their mind and back out of the deal.

Maybe your prospects told their current accountant, attorney, or engineer that they were moving their business to you. If that were to happen, do you think your competitor would just give up, or do you think they would say or do whatever it took to keep the business? Do you think that it is possible your competition would talk them out of making the move by dropping their price or promising to do better?

As a result, your new client is now a "unclient."

Perhaps the client is having second thoughts about risking a change, or he is afraid that he will be paying too much. If your prospects have thoughts of backing out of doing business with you, you want that to happen while you are still in front of them rather than over the phone — or worse, by email or voicemail!

CASE IN POINT

An accounting firm we were working with was frustrated because they were having good meetings with prospects, the prospects were agreeing to work with them, and then those prospects would back out of the deal at the last second.

We had this accounting firm do some research, and they found that they were trying to take business away from the same competitor over and over again. When they were finally able to get one of their prospects who backed out of a deal on the phone, that prospect admitted that the incumbent accounting firm scared him by telling him how much time it would take to transfer all of the data to a new firm, and that they would hear of problems in the past when people had moved their accounting to them.

In addition, the incumbent firm promised to lower their rates and have partners give the prospect more attention. If that accounting firm who lost the deal was aware that those issues might come up, do you think that they could have prepared their new client for what he might hear from the incumbent firm, who was desperate to keep the business? Do you think they could have approached the end of the meeting differently?

THE POST-SELL

The purpose of the Post-Sell Step is two-fold. You want to lock up the business while also setting the stage for future referrals. So, once you have closed the business, you want to thank your prospect and then bring up minor compromises, as long as they are minor and have nothing to do with price.

At this point, you want to make sure that your competition does not undo what you have just worked so hard to close!

You need to ask what, if anything, might cause the decision maker(s) to change course. You need to prepare your new client for the desperate pleas that he will hear from your competitors when he find out that the business went to you. You need to ask your new client if he would like you to help him prepare for the pressure he will receive from the incumbent firm by rehearsing with him what he can say when he gets that phone call or request to meet.

The accounting firm client that we mentioned in the above story changed their tactics once they started working with us. They began incorporating a post-sell discussion — and you need to do the same!

Our client warned their prospects that they might hear things like the incumbent firm exaggerating the amount of time it would take to switch firms, or making up stories regarding the difficulty of switching, or even offering to drop their rates. Our client had several of their current clients write letters discussing how easy the transition was from their old accounting firm to the new accounting firm. These letters also discussed the positive interactions they were having with the partners of their new firm. Finally, our client asked if it would be helpful for them to be involved when it was time to call the incumbent firm to discuss what was needed to make the switch.

Almost overnight, our client stopped losing prospects who had committed to them.

UP-FRONT CONTRACT

Once the issue of the incumbent firm is addressed, establish an up-front contract regarding exactly what happens next with your new client. You do not want anything to fall through the cracks!

Make sure you discuss the information you need to get next from your prospect, and in what time frame you need to receive it. Share with your client the steps you will be taking on your side. If someone is being transitioned to another professional in your firm, you must help that person to make a smooth transition.

Once someone becomes a client, the two of you must be on the same page at all times!

REFERRALS

The last part of the Post-Sell Step is to set the expectations that you will be asking for referrals as your relationship grows.

Our experience is that your prospects will be very comfortable with you once they have gone through the business development process, and they will be open to discussing future opportunities with you once they experience what it is like to work with you.

If you set the expectation early in the relationship that you will be asking for referrals in the future, the amount of referrals you receive once you do ask will greatly increase — so set the stage. Do not let your own personal "head trash" about asking for referrals get in the way of asking your clients — old and new — for referrals.

When done correctly, the Fulfillment and Post-Sell Steps will ensure that you not only give an effective and on-point presentation, but these steps will also help you to grow your business by setting the stage for a steady influx of referrals.

We have covered a lot of material in these previous chapters. In the next chapter we will talk a bit about putting it all together.

Recap: Post-Sell

- The Post-Sell Step is not optional. It is a mandatory part of the professional business development process.
- The purpose of the Post-Sell Step is two-fold. You want to lock up the business while also setting the stage for future referrals.
- Directly address, in person, all the issues that might cause the decision maker(s) to change course.
- Your prospects will be very comfortable with you once they have gone through the business development process, and they will be open to discussing future opportunities with you once they experience what it is like to work with you.

CHAPTER TWENTY-FOUR

Using the System to Develop and Expand Your Base of Business

"If you think you can do a thing or think you can't do a thing, you are right."

HENRY FORD

"Anyone who stops learning is old, whether at 20 or 80. Anyone who keeps learning stays young. The greatest thing in life is to keep your mind young."

HENRY FORD

I t is possible you have evidence to support the belief that you cannot succeed in business development. You may have never tried because it was too far outside of your comfort zone — or you tried once and failed, so you vowed to never attempt to develop business again.

If you have a self-limiting mindset, there is not a book or program in existence that will help you become a rainmaker.

It is also possible that you are excited to have a starting point or an

163

additional resource to help you along the road to becoming a successful rainmaker. Reading this book is just a small part of what you need to do to begin to develop your own book of business, or to increase the book of business that you have already earned.

It took you many years to become an expert in your chosen field. It required dedication to learn and practice, and a willingness to learn from your mistakes. Business development is also a learned skill and can be developed and improved over time.

To become successful in business development, it will take a commitment to move out of your comfort zone in order to try something new, a willingness to fail and learn from your mistakes when practicing these tactics and techniques, a commitment to schedule time to participate in business development activities, and the dedication to learn a new system.

CASE IN POINT

One of our clients is an intellectual property attorney named Barbara. Though she was a senior attorney who was very good at her work, Barbara's managing partner very strongly recommended that she give us a call because she had never developed any business, and therefore was not being considered for partnership. When we first sat down with Barbara she was very resistant and admitted that she was not very comfortable talking to other people. Barbara's entire business development effort consisted of publishing a few articles.

Initially, Barbara was unsure about working with us, but she knew that she may not last at her firm if she did not start to develop some of her own clients. She was forced to move out of her comfort zone because she did not want to leave her current firm, and she was committed to doing whatever it took to be successful in business development.

We gave Barbara an assessment, and then met with her to discuss her strengths and weaknesses. We worked together with Barbara to create a prospecting plan that was slightly outside of her comfort zone, but included activities that she was willing to try. Barbara became more comfortable once she learned that there was a process and a system to fall back on both for prospecting and for meeting with potential clients.

After working together for one year, Barbara went from no new business generation to $500,000 in new business generation.

Three years later, Barbara was the top producer of new clients and new revenue in her practice area.

What Do You Want?

The best place to start your journey is to set good goals for yourself. Where would you like your personal business to be in the next six months, one year, five years, and beyond?

It is impossible to determine your success if you do not identify what you want to accomplish.

When setting your goals, make sure that you are setting SMART goals. Commit to the process that you are going to utilize to track your progress. Create a cookbook that will allow you to track your behavior to ensure that you will achieve your goals.

How Will You Do It?

Once you have set your goals, create a prospecting plan that will force you to participate in the behaviors necessary to achieve your goals. Identify your targets (both size of company and industry), commit to a certain amount of prospecting behavior on a daily, weekly, and monthly basis, determine your budget for prospecting and marketing, and choose the prospecting activities that will give you the greatest chance to achieve your goals.

Make sure that you are tracking the return on investment for all of your prospecting activities, and make changes if you are not on track to accomplish your goals.

Make a Plan

Next, commit to a system of business development that allows you to take control of the process and better predict the outcome of your meetings. It is time to stop "winging it" or "flying by the seat of your pants," and to start utilizing the seven steps of the Sandler Selling System.

You need to overcome the overwhelming desire to show off your expertise and provide free consulting.

Set an up-front contract with your prospects, so that there is no "mutual mystification" to ensure that you and your prospect are on the same page at all times.

Qualify your opportunities by uncovering the prospect's pain and determining how his pain is impacting his business — or better yet, him.

What is costing the prospect time and money? Where is his potential liability? What will the impact be if he does not fix his problems?

Go beyond the pain indicators and uncover the real pain.

Identify how your prospect is going to make his decision. Is he the sole decision maker, or does he have to run it by someone else? Are the decisions made locally or elsewhere? When was he hoping to make the decision and implement the solutions?

Only provide your expertise to a prospect you have qualified.

Make sure that you address the prospect's pain in the Fulfillment Step, rather than giving a standard presentation or proposal.

If your prospect agrees to move forward, do not forget to do a Post-Sell Step to make sure that someone does not back out of the deal at the end of the process.

PATIENCE AND COMMITMENT

All of these changes take time. There is no magic potion that is going to turn you into a business development machine overnight. Typically, our clients work with us for one year or longer before they have internalized their new beliefs, fine-tuned their prospecting plan to optimize their results, and mastered the Sandler Selling System.

If you implement the concepts we have introduced in this book, you will start to see results in 30 to 60 days, but it takes ongoing training, coaching, and reinforcement over time to make permanent, positive changes.

The most successful business development professionals participate in ongoing training and utilize a personal business coach. A business coach will help you to customize a business development plan, based on your strengths and weaknesses, and hold you accountable for the behaviors that you commit to do as part of your plan. A coach will encourage you to move outside of your comfort zone and help you adapt the Sandler Selling System to match your industry and to accommodate your personality.

On the last page of this book you will find instructions to receive one free Sandler Training® class. Use it!

Now is the time to take the next step and *commit* to your success in business development.

David Sandler, creator of the Sandler Selling System, had a favorite saying, as important for its invocation of the principle of repetition and reinforcement as it was for what it actually instructed: *Do the behaviors! Do the behaviors! Do the behaviors!*

With that sound advice in mind, what are the actions you are going to commit to taking, and repeating, as a result of the concepts that you have learned in this book?

Recap: To be successful in business development you need:

- A commitment to move out of your comfort zone in order to try something new.
- A willingness to fail and learn from your mistakes when practicing these tactics and techniques.
- A commitment to schedule time to participate in business development activities.
- The dedication to learn a new system.
- Willingness to *do the behaviors.*

ABOUT THE AUTHORS

CHUCK AND EVAN POLIN are a father-son training team, located in the metropolitan Philadelphia, Pennsylvania market, with more than two decades of experience in the Sandler Training organization.

CHUCK POLIN is CEO of The Training Resource Group, Inc., an authorized Sandler Training Center in Philadelphia, Pennsylvania. He has been a Sandler Trainer for more than 20 years, and brings over 40 years of sales, sales management and corporate executive experience to the firm. Before opening his Sandler Training Center in 1994, Chuck spent the majority of his career in the women's apparel industry in New York City, where he managed sales forces, directed marketing campaigns, and was President of a Fortune 500 company division. In 2009, Chuck was named "Small Business Person of the Year" by The Greater Philadelphia Chamber of Commerce.

EVAN POLIN is President of The Training Resource Group, Inc. He joined the firm in 2001 and brings a wealth of training and coaching experience to his clients, providing business development workshops for Bar Associations, the AIA, University Alumni Associations, Chambers of Commerce, and Professional Associations. He teaches professionals a process that focuses on identifying pain, generating more referrals, targeting accounts, differentiating their firm from the competition, and effectively qualifying and disqualifying prospects. Before joining The Training Resource Group, Evan earned a master's degree at The University of Pennsylvania; after graduation he became an Employee Assistance Professional (EAP), working at Amtrak and United Health Care. Evan has spoken at national and regional conferences, provided training programs for Fortune 500 companies, and provided Critical Incident Stress Debriefings for companies in New York City and northern New Jersey after the terrorist attacks on September 11, 2001.

Sandler Training is a worldwide provider of coaching, consultative sales, leadership and management training programs with over 250 offices around the world.

CONGRATULATIONS!

Selling Professional Services The Sandler Way

includes a complimentary seminar!

Take this opportunity to personally experience the non-traditional sales training and reinforcement coaching that has been recognized internationally for decades.

Companies in the Fortune 1000 as well as thousands of small- to medium-sized businesses choose Sandler Training for sales, leadership, management, and a wealth of other skill-building programs. Now, it's your turn, and it's free!

You'll learn the latest practical, tactical, feet-in-the-street sales methods directly from your neighborhood Sandler trainers! They're knowledgeable, friendly, and informed about your local selling environment.

Here's how you redeem YOUR FREE SEMINAR invitation.

1. Go to www.Sandler.com and click on the LOCATE A TRAINING CENTER button (upper right corner).
2. Select your location from the drop-down menus.
3. Review the list of all the Sandler trainers in your area.
4. Call your local Sandler trainer, mention *Selling Professional Services The Sandler Way*, and reserve your place at the next seminar!